With surgical precision, careful exeg
spun illustrations, R. T. Kendall no
wrong with so much of today's relig
promised, corrupt, and superficial i
paints a beautiful picture of what authentic, Jesus-centered,
Spirit-empowered religion looks like. The dove instead of
the pigeon!

R. T. Kendall has expressed the cry of every hungry soul
for the real thing. Nothing halfway, nothing cheap, no imi-
tations, but only the power of the Holy Spirit to bring us
incomparable righteousness, peace, and joy as God Himself sets up His throne in our hearts. We must distinguish
between pigeons and doves, and RT does so for us in a most
lively, natural, joyful, and helpful way. Read it!

It is a great joy to call R. T. Kendall a true personal friend! I
have the greatest respect for him and his ministry. His book
Pigeon Religion will be a huge help to all who are seekers
of divine truth! His comparisons of the counterfeit and the
genuine moves of the Holy Spirit are priceless. You will be
inspired and challenged to dig deeper into the Word of God.
This book will aid you in your quest to draw ever closer to
Holy Spirit.

As perhaps no one else I know, RT is passionate for the religion of the dove and keen to avoid all forms of what he calls
"pigeon religion." While some pursue the dove, too many
settle for the pigeon. As in nature so in the things of the

Spirit, some say there is no difference between the dove and the pigeon, but if you have ever been in the presence of *the* Dove, you know there is. Many are quick to judge what is or is not of God, and each one of us may draw the line in different places. But RT offers some simple guidelines to help us all discern correctly. He combines practical common sense, heart-warming openness to the Holy Spirit, and total confidence in the finality of Scripture. This is a book for our times and, as I dare to believe, a book that can prepare us for the visitations of the divine Dove that lie ahead.

—Rev. Colin Dye
Senior Minister, Kensington Temple
London, England

I first heard the "pigeon religion" concept in a sermon RT preached in Westminster Chapel, London, and I sat riveted to my seat. What he explained was frighteningly real. The deception was everywhere. From soaring cathedrals and booming organ music to backstreet churches and tambourines, "pigeon religion" permeates much more than we dare to think. Thankfully, this message of correction is now before us in print. Read it! Do it!

—Charles Carrin

When R. T. Kendall writes a book (which is often), illustrating takes on new meaning. He has the ability to mine a vein of gold and draw out every particle of value to support the truth under observation. This unique approach with references to natural and familiar world knowledge may prove to be among his best sellers. It is bound to yield valued truth under new light.

—Jack Taylor
Dimensions Ministries
Melbourne, Florida

This delightful, edifying, and encouraging book invites us to a deeper appreciation for the Holy Spirit. With a solid balance of Word and Spirit, R. T. Kendall writes about the Spirit in a way that makes us want to experience the Spirit more deeply and recognize God's ways.

—DR. CRAIG KEENER

RT has written a whole book pointing to the differences between the dove and the pigeon, biologically similar but "spiritually" so different. As he often does, RT has pioneered a line of thought worth exploring.

—DR. MICHAEL EATON

Pigeon Religion brings to light some challenging topics, thought-provoking questions, and scriptural answers. As always, Dr. Kendall provides clear teaching that illustrates the importance of being led by the authentic Holy Spirit, in contrast to being misled by a counterfeit. I earnestly pray this book opens your eyes and ministers to your heart the way it did to mine.

—PASTOR BILL WILSON, PhD
METRO WORLD CHILD

R. T. Kendall is one of my favorite writers. His new book *Pigeon Religion* is to be added to his many great books. I am sure many will find it edifying and insightful. Well done, RT. An excellent book on spirituality and discernment. A needed book for our time. I enjoyed it and was challenged by its message in a good way.

—RANDY CLARK, DMin
FOUNDER AND PRESIDENT, GLOBAL AWAKENING AND THE
APOSTOLIC NETWORK OF GLOBAL AWAKENING

In a day when pigeon religion seems to be flourishing, there are many who long for the dove to come, the obviousness of enjoying God's manifest approval on their ministries. Such a timely word to keep us on track pursuing God with a purity of heart. This is vintage R. T. Kendall at his best.

—GRANT BREWSTER
PASTOR, ISLAND CHURCH
BAINBRIDGE ISLAND, WASHINGTON

It is no surprise that Dr. R. T. Kendall has taken an abiding biblical symbol, the dove, and used its counterpoint, the pigeon, as a doorway to new meaning. Our faith is not just cognitive; it is also imaginative. From his platform as one of the most respected authors in the global evangelical church, RT hands you a book that is both confrontational and compassionate, confessional and collaborative. This book heals as it wounds. There is some pigeon in the best of us, but the dove beckons. Enjoy these rare insights.

—JOEL C. GREGORY
PROFESSOR OF PREACHING, BAYLOR'S GEORGE W. TRUETT
THEOLOGICAL SEMINARY

Pigeon Religion:

Holy Spirit,
IS THAT YOU?

R. T. KENDALL

CHARISMA
HOUSE

Library of Congress Cataloging-in-Publication Data:
Names: Kendall, R. T., 1935- author.
Title: Pigeon religion : Holy Spirit, is that you? / R.T.
Kendall.
Description: First edition. | Lake Mary : Charisma House,
2016. | Includes
    bibliographical references and index.
Identifiers: LCCN 2016006573| ISBN 9781629987194 (trade
paper : alk. paper) |
    ISBN 9781629987200 (e-book)
Subjects: LCSH: Holy Spirit. | Discernment (Christian
theology)
Classification: LCC BT121.3 .K457 2016 | DDC 231/.3--dc23
LC record available at http://lccn.loc.gov/2016006573

16 17 18 19 20 — 9 8 7 6 5 4 3 2
Printed in the United States of America

To Pete and Melissa

WOUNDED DOVE

A wounded dove was put in my pigeon cote,
And what I saw I wrote

A loving dove so tender,
Put in with loud and raucous birds to mend there;

The pigeons were quieted by her gentle coo,
And the love she gave as only doves can do,

The fighting among them ceased,
And the whole cote lived in peace.

Then as her wings healed and she said goodbye;
The pigeons sadly watched as she took to the sky;

I want to learn from this dove with gentle coo
And learn to love like doves do;

To have a soft voice that turns away wrath,
And in every relation leave love in the aftermath,

And when the wings of my soul are healed and I
    say goodbye,
May those who know me, know, at last I'm free in
    God's blue sky.

                       —BILL G. "PETE" CANTRELL

CONTENTS

FOREWORD

———— ◆ ————

I N MAY 2015 my wife and I helped lead a retreat for ministers in the Smoky Mountains of Tennessee. I knew most of the couples who were joining us, but I was surprised to learn that one of the attendees was Sally Fesperman, a leader (with her late husband, Jay) during the early days of the charismatic renewal of the 1960s and 1970s.

Sally is eighty-eight, but she is as bright-eyed and energetic as any twentysomething I know. She loves to talk about her relationship with Jesus, and she shared many stories about the early days of renewal when thousands of Baptists, Methodists, Episcopalians, and Presbyterians were discovering the baptism in the Holy Spirit. Sally brought back so many memories of the mid-1970s, when I was filled with the Spirit as a teenager.

While in the mountains for the May retreat, God spoke to me from Isaiah 35 about another wave of the Holy Spirit that is coming soon. He told me, from verse 6 (NAS): "Waters will break forth in the wilderness." I have never been more convinced that God is going to refresh us again with a sudden outpouring of His presence and power. I was so excited about this promise that I asked Sally one morning to pray over us, and to prophetically pass the torch of renewal to the younger generation.

I wept when Sally prayed over us because I am desperate

to see revival. However, by the last day of the retreat I was sobered by the responsibility of receiving this torch of renewal. That's because I know that when the Holy Spirit was poured out on the American church more than forty years ago, we mishandled this precious gift.

For many years, Bible teacher R. T. Kendall has been a lone voice in the wilderness. He was touched by the charismatic renewal while pastoring in England, but he has always called the church to treat the Holy Spirit with respect and to use the Spirit's gifts with integrity. He has warned us often that the Spirit can be grieved and quenched because of our flippant disregard for His sensitivity. I share Kendall's burden. That's why I was excited to hear of this book. If we do not learn to carry the anointing of the Holy Spirit properly, we could end up like Uzzah, who thought he could control the presence of God any way he wanted. (See 2 Samuel 6:1–11.) David learned a hard lesson when Uzzah died; yet we tend to forget that we can't treat God's holy things with such irreverence.

Here are five ways we mishandled the outpouring of the Spirit in the last season:

1. We exploited it. The first attempt at quenching the Spirit's power in the New Testament church was made by Ananias and Sapphira, who were full of greed (see Acts 5:1–11). The same thing happened to the charismatic movement in the 1980s, when prosperity preachers with dollar signs in their eyes showed up to merchandise the Spirit's anointing. Swaggering evangelists in white suits and Rolexes began pushing people to the floor and convincing crowds to dig into their wallets to give in "miracle" offerings. And so began the slow but steady sellout. We didn't realize the greed was driving us further and further from the Spirit's blessing.

2. We fabricated it. In the early days of renewal, charismatic leaders had a sense of holy awe when they prayed for people. They didn't want to do anything to grieve the Spirit. But somewhere along the way, some ministers realized they could fake the gifts of the Holy Spirit and still draw a crowd. Charlatans began hosting charismatic sideshows, complete with faked healings, spooky stage drama, and mesmerizing manipulation. God's holy anointing was replaced by mood music and a quivering voice. Anybody with discernment could sense that the Spirit's sweet presence had exited the building.

3. We corrupted it. In the early charismatic days, I cut my spiritual teeth on meaty messages from firebrands such as Judson Cornwall, Leonard Ravenhill, Corrie ten Boom, Keith Green, Derek Prince, Joy Dawson, and Winkey Pratney. They preached regularly about the fear of God. Their messages demanded holiness. But if you fast-forward to today, you will find that much of the preaching in our movement has been reduced to drivel. It is sad that people can attend a "Spirit-filled" church today and never hear a sermon explaining that fornication is a sin. It is sadder that we have preachers in our pulpits who shamelessly flaunt sexual sin under the banner of a cheap grace message that will actually send people to hell.

4. We denominationalized it. When the Holy Spirit fell on certain groups in previous decades, their leaders assumed that the blessing of God was an indication that they were "special." Some denominations even taught that all other Christians would one day come under their group's banner—because they believed they had elite status. Sectarian pride might sound spiritual, but it is still pride. And don't ever think that nondenominational church networks are immune to this virus. There are trendy new groups today that claim to have a corner on truth. Their subtle message is, "We are better." Don't let this smug attitude quench the Holy Spirit.

5. We professionalized it. In the early days of charismatic renewal, there was a sense of childlike wonder as people discovered the power of the Spirit for the first time. The meetings were Christ-centered, the sermons were solidly biblical, and the fellowship was deep. We could sing "They Will Know

We Are Christians by Our Love" because we felt a deep bond with each other in the Holy Spirit. But it didn't take long to replace the genuine sense of New Testament *koinonia* with something colder and less inviting. We began emphasizing titles. We discovered slick marketing techniques. Churches and their budgets grew. Then a funny thing happened on the way to the megachurch: we lost our simplicity. We turned church into a business. We stopped being relational and we became professional.

I'm not against growth, megachurches, or marketing. The Holy Spirit can produce and direct all those things! But if we sacrifice the freshness and warmth of relationships on the altar of professional Christianity, we may discover the Holy Spirit has withdrawn from our ministries.

May the Lord help us to cultivate an atmosphere that attracts His presence rather than repels Him. I believe this excellent book by R. T. Kendall will help us carry the ark of God's presence more carefully. May we be ready to receive the baton as a younger generation embraces the promise of another move of God. Come, Holy Spirit!

—J. LEE GRADY
FORMER EDITOR, *CHARISMA* MAGAZINE
DIRECTOR, THE MORDECAI PROJECT

PREFACE

Y OU MAY LAUGH at the title, but this is a no-joke book. The premise of this book is that the dove is the symbol of the Holy Spirit and the pigeon the symbol of the counterfeit spirit. It illustrates the comparison between a diet of milk, which produces a superficial, carnal, or "worldly" Christian, as opposed to solid food, which is for the mature (1 Cor. 3:2–3; Heb. 5:12–14).

"In the multitude of counselors there is safety" (Prov. 11:14). I have sought the opinion of all I could find in the preparation of this book. The greatest caution from my friends has been to beware of being too negative. If I am not careful, this book could be pigeon religion itself, the last thing on earth I want! And yet I am convinced that the warning contained in this book is needed at the present time. I hope it will spare many innocent, sincere people from being taken in by pigeon religion, believing they are hearing from God when they are not. It is so easy to make a mistake in this area. After all, Satan masquerades as an angel of light (2 Cor. 11:14).

I dedicate this book to Pete and Melissa Cantrell. I will have more to say about Pete in this book. I am also indebted to a number of friends who have kindly offered their criticisms; among them are Joy Strang and my UK friends Lyndon Bowring and Rob Parsons. I thank especially Dr. Ann Allen Salter, a veterinarian in Montgomery, Alabama, for her very relevant knowledge about pigeons and doves. I am so grateful to Lee Grady, former editor of *Charisma*, for his gracious foreword. My editor, Debbie Marrie, has been exceptionally helpful in the production of this book. But I am most grateful as always for the cautions, help, and encouragement from my wife, Louise.

—R. T. Kendall
Hendersonville, Tennessee
September 2015

INTRODUCTION

———◆———

I WILL NEVER FORGET one of my first visits to the Western Wall (known as the "Wailing Wall") in Jerusalem. A young Jewish man was giving me a bit of its history. I well recall reading about how the day the Six-Day War ended, Jews from all over Jerusalem—and eventually all over the world—flooded the area of the Western Wall. I was excited to learn all I could. I was there as part of a seminary class in archaeology I was taking at the time.

The young man pointed out that you can sometimes see a dove in one of the crevices of the Western Wall. This, to him, was a sign of peace.

As I looked at the historic wall and reflected on his words, lo and behold, there came a dove into one of the crevices. I was so pleased to be witnessing this rare and precious sight. I took a photograph and included an enlarged copy of it when I turned in my paper on the Messianic Hope of Modern Israel, focusing on the Western Wall. I was so proud of that photo. That is, until my archaeology professor pointed out to me that my dove was in fact...a pigeon.

Years later, this embarrassing experience became part of the inspiration for one of my books. My old friend Pete Cantrell had just fetched Louise and me at the Will Rogers Airport in Oklahoma City, Oklahoma. His church—First Baptist Church of Ada, Oklahoma—had invited Jack Taylor and me to do a weekend meeting called "Word and Spirit Conference." On the way to Ada, I casually mentioned to

Pete that I was finishing a book called *Sensitivity of the Spirit*. I had a hunch that he might help me, given his experience with doves and pigeons. I certainly knew of Pete's interest in pigeons and doves but was not prepared for what followed. I said to him, "I have a theory that there is a huge difference between pigeons and doves, but nobody agrees with me."

At that time my notion was in its embryonic form, namely that whereas the dove is a symbol of the Holy Spirit, the pigeon might be regarded in some sense as a symbol of the counterfeit spirit. I had been developing this notion ever since my mistake at the Western Wall, and I had done some research. I was aware that pigeons and doves are of the same ornithological family and that they are sometimes used interchangeably in the original biblical languages.

In my research I had discovered that ornithologists state categorically that there is no difference between a pigeon and a dove. I talked with the top authority at the British Museum in London on this matter. He was dogmatic. "There is no difference between a pigeon and a dove," he said somewhat bluntly to me. I felt so disappointed because I was convinced there was a difference. He gave me the name and phone number of the top authority on this subject in the United States, a professor at the University of Iowa. I valued the privilege of talking with this man too, but the reply was the same: "There is no difference between a pigeon and a dove." I felt even more disappointed. Maybe a little stupid too. Who was I—a mere Bible teacher—to go against world-class scientists whose job it is to know about these things?

That weekend in Oklahoma, Pete and I were watching a religious program. I am always cheered when I hear the gospel preached on television, and I have frequently had the opportunity myself to share the Word of God through this medium. But this time the program was not about proclaiming the gospel but instead was almost entirely devoted to giving money to this man's ministry. The preacher went to extremes in guaranteeing that I would absolutely prosper financially if I sent money to him. And yet what capped it all was a portrait of a white dove at the end of the show. I found myself saying, "*This is pigeon religion.*"

I told Pete my idea about "pigeon religion" followed by my dilemma over what the scientists had stated about pigeons and doves. At first he agreed with the scientists, reinforcing that there is no difference between a pigeon and a dove. "A pigeon is nothing more than a fat dove," he said. But I pressed him with my theory, and suddenly it was like turning on a thousand volts of electricity. "I see what you mean, RT," he said, his mind racing like lightning. "It's true that doves and pigeons are the same *anatomically*, but there is a big difference between a pigeon and a dove *temperamentally.*"

Pete Cantrell, now aged eighty-five, has spent over sixty-five years training pigeons and raising doves: studying, playing with, and carefully observing both pigeons and doves. "My middle name is Grayson; I was named after the Grayson dove," he said to me. Although an oilman by trade and profession, Pete's lifelong hobby has been raising thousands of pigeons and doves at his estate. When I contemplate the likelihood of my finding anybody in the whole world who has given so much attention to pigeons and doves, I can't believe my luck (if you will pardon the expression).

That weekend in Ada, once Pete saw what I was getting at, his mind began churning out information like a computer. I finished my book *Sensitivity of the Spirit* a few weeks later, which includes a chapter showing the differences between pigeons and doves.

Over the years since writing *Sensitivity of the Spirit*, I have been urged by a number of friends to enlarge upon this idea. One reason for my hesitation is that the book could almost by definition be partly negative. I am loath to write a negative book. It is my earnest prayer that I will be humble and as Christlike as I possibly can in writing this book. This is because I felt the time had come to turn this analogy into an entire book, hoping indeed that it would be a blessing. It is my aim to be positive and yet lovingly call attention to some trends and assumptions in our day. I call this *Pigeon Religion*—my term for practices that are thought to be Spirit-led but are not rooted in Holy Scripture.

While working on this new book, I decided to google the question: "Is there a difference between a pigeon and a dove?" A lively Internet discussion turned up in my search results. What interested me most was that nobody was laughing at the question. People were saying things such as pigeons—not doves—are among the most "unpeaceful" birds around. That alone suggested at least one huge difference between pigeons and doves. That is only the beginning. It is the dove—not the pigeon—that has become the symbol of peace.

I've also received even more information about pigeons and doves from one of the readers of *Sensitivity of the Spirit*, Dr. Ann Allen Salter, a veterinarian in Montgomery, Alabama. I have been amazed and helped by the information she too has kindly provided for the present book.

For those who care to go into this deeply, it will be soon discovered that there are many, many kinds of pigeons and many kinds of doves. But generally speaking the differences are the same, whether one speaks of the feral pigeon or the turtledove. In a word: we can learn a few things from pigeons and doves and how their differences in particular might be applied to us.

DEFINITION OF "PIGEON RELIGION"

Here is my definition of "pigeon religion": it is the encroachment of any teaching, ministry, or practice that you thought was a dove—the authentic Holy Spirit—but which turned out to be a pigeon—the counterfeit. In a word: the flesh, not the Spirit. What initially looks like a dove but turns out to be a pigeon is "pigeon religion."

Like any analogy or comparison, one can push the metaphor too far. I shall try to avoid this. Here are, generally speaking, the temperamental differences between pigeons and doves:

PIGEONS	DOVES (ESPECIALLY TURTLEDOVES)
Fight with each other	Never fight with each other
Belligerent	Peaceful
Noisy	Quiet
Not bothered by noise or people	Hypersensitive; hate noise
Love attention	Don't love attention
Take themselves very seriously	Don't take themselves seriously
Greedy	Not greedy
Aggressive	Not aggressive
Get dependent on man for food	Find their own food
Eat anything (junk food)	Eat only seeds or fruit
Droppings carry dangerous fungi	Droppings not so dangerous
Territorial	Not territorial
Protect their nest	Do not protect their nest
Fly high (one thousand feet or more)	Fly no more than thirty feet high
Gregarious; fly as a group	Fly solo or in pairs
Unafraid of humans	Afraid of humans
Can be trained or domesticated	Cannot be trained
Homing instinct (will return to a cage)	Will only return for survival
Can have more than one mate	One mate for life

I do not intend to build this book on every single difference between pigeons and doves. The reader may want to have some fun doing that. You will no doubt see things I had not thought of. In any case, not all of these differences are particularly relevant for us. I have barely scratched the surface when I consider the subjects and relevant issues that could be brought up. Moreover, the above list could be extended. But some of these differences are so striking that they deserve comment at various stages in this book. There are no doubt some exceptions. I have heard some reports of doves being trained, but I am not sure to what extent this may be common—if true. Remember too—like parables that do not stand "on all four legs," you can, I repeat, push the distinctions too far. I am not basing my views on science nor am I building a theology on these observations. I am simply fascinated by the temperamental differences between pigeons and doves as described above. Some of them are striking if not amazing.

Among other goals, I hope this book will help us laugh at ourselves. After all, if we can't laugh at ourselves, we are in pretty bad shape! People who take themselves too seriously cannot laugh at themselves, nor can they abide any hint that suggests a criticism. We all have a lot to learn. I want this book to help teach us to *think*, and that we might develop into a greater maturity as a result. My mentor, Dr. Martyn Lloyd-Jones, used to say that the Christian faith should teach us "how to think."

Jesus rebuked the Pharisees and Sadducees for their lack of discernment. "You know how to interpret the appearance of the sky, but you cannot interpret the signs of the times" (Matt. 16:3, AMPC). Paul warned that in the last days:

> For the time will come when people will not endure
> sound doctrine, but they will gather to themselves
> teachers in accordance with their own desires,

> having itching ears, and they will turn their ears
> away from the truth and turn to myths.
> —2 TIMOTHY 4:3–4

It is my opinion that the time Paul warned about has come. This book seeks to address this trend. Is it possible that *you* have sought out a teacher or leader simply because they tell you what you *want* to hear—not what you *should* hear?

At a previous residence we had lovely neighbors who would sometimes come to hear me preach. But most of the time they preferred to stay in and watch their favorite preacher on television. They added: "This way we don't have to get dressed for church, we can smoke our cigarettes and drink our martinis while we watch, and, what is more, he *always* makes us feel *so good*." We liked these neighbors a lot and they were very fond of us. But my preaching did not always succeed in making them feel good. However, their favorite TV preacher always did.

What worries me is that many people are taken in not by a ministry that upholds the truth and changes lives but only by what makes them feel better. It would appear that their aim in going to church is to come out feeling better—especially if no repentance or change of lifestyle is required.

C. S. Lewis said, "I believe there are many accommodating preachers, and too many practitioners in the church who are not believers. Jesus Christ did not say "Go into all the world and tell the world that it is quite right."[1]

Some of these leaders say things that appeal to one's love for the Bible. "This is my Bible; I believe what it says" gets the attention of sincere people who feel comfortable thinking they are going to hear from God. Sometimes what is preached is partly true. But what is even more troublesome is that it is not merely a case of "black and white." This means not only are we talking about "gray" areas but that there is a little bit of the counterfeit *and* the real in some of these teachers. Neither are we implying that those who propagate error are always unconverted people. I think it is possible for truly regenerate people to get off the rails theologically. Or even to preach to tickle the ears of their hearers. After all, none of us is perfect.

BONEFISHING AND THE HOLY SPIRIT

I now bring in a different example: bonefishing. Do bear with me in this section if you are not too interested in fishing. Bonefishing parallels the quest to recognize doves from pigeons. When I look for bonefish, I need to differentiate the real from the counterfeit—since certain other fish look like bonefish.

For many years my hobby has been bonefishing. It is essentially a sport. You don't normally eat bonefish—they are too bony. The Latin name is *Albula vulpes*—white fox. The bonefish is a wily fish—very hard to catch—that swims in tropical waters of the world, as in the Florida Keys and the Bahamas. They are normally caught in shallow water—knee deep (twelve to fifteen inches) is perfect. Bonefishing combines hunting and fishing; you *look* for them and hopefully spot them before you cast to them. I have introduced dozens of friends to bonefishing, most recently my friend the late John Paul Jackson.

I began reading about bonefishing in 1964. For some reason I was immediately fascinated. I was cautioned, however—don't try it without a guide to help you find them. You need a guide for two reasons: to pole (punting) the boat and to help you find them. I went to a fishing camp in Jewfish Creek in Key Largo. I said to the manager, "I want to go bonefishing. Will you rent me a boat?"

He replied, "Do you have a guide?"

"No," I said.

"Sir, are you a bonefisherman?"

"I will be after today."

"Have you ever been bonefishing before?"

"No sir."

"Let me explain: nobody—no one—ever goes bonefishing for the first time without a guide."

I was sure I did not need a guide. For one thing, I did not want to pay the fee (not cheap), and I did not want to admit I *needed* a guide. I simply said to the manager, "Will you rent me a boat?"

"Certainly."

"Would you show me on a map where to go?"

"Certainly. Head out Barnes Sound for about twenty minutes, come to the cut that leads to Largo Sound. Bonefish are on the other side of Largo Sound. Good luck."

I came back some eight hours later. "How many did you catch?" the manager asked. "There weren't any," I replied. Someone overhearing the conversation said, "I saw you in Largo Sound. There were fish all around you." Almost humiliated at my failure, I left and vowed never to do that again.

However, I read a few more articles in fishing magazines and knew what I had done wrong. I returned to the same fishing camp and went to the same spot—looking everywhere for bonefish. I saw none. Everybody seemed to catch them but me.

Months later, swallowing my pride, I yielded to the idea of a guide. He said, "Meet me at Mayo's Fishing Camp in Largo Sound." I thought to myself, "This guide doesn't know what he is doing. There are no fish there." We met at eight o'clock on June 1, 1965. I will never forget it. He headed us in his boat directly to the *same spot* where I had looked in vain for months and months. Within minutes he whispered, "Look carefully, eleven o'clock, eighty feet. Huge bonefish. Eight to ten pounds."

"Where?" I asked.

"Too late, he's gone." But minutes later, the guide calmly said, "Twelve o'clock. Moving to one, now two o'clock."

"Oh," I moaned. "So *that's* a bonefish." The fish—by dozens—had been in the same area the whole time. They had been under my nose but I could not see them. Before the day was over, I hooked five bonefish. I could not do it without the guide, however.

Jesus said of the Holy Spirit that He would "guide" us into all truth (John 16:13). The work of the Holy Spirit is to reveal what is *there*. Right there in the Word. Under our nose. Paul said that the natural man does not receive the things of the Spirit of God because they are "foolishness" to him. The natural man cannot understand them "because they are spiritually discerned" (1 Cor. 2:14). The natural man assumes he can read and understand the Bible because he reads and grasps literature, philosophy, architecture, psychology, and even theology. Therefore, when he picks up the Bible he assumes he will understand it. He cannot! The Bible is not an ordinary book. It is a spiritual—supernatural—book. You cannot understand the Bible without a *guide*—the Holy Spirit. The truth is right there—it is all around you. Yes, under your nose. But without the Holy Spirit to *show* what is there, you will see nothing!

Spiritual discernment. That is what *Pigeon Religion* is about. It is by the guidance of the Holy Spirit that we see what is there. And what is *not* there. Also, what needs to be avoided.

To return to my bonefishing memories, one of the first things to look out for when pursuing bonefish are the counterfeit fish that swim in the shallow waters. Not all fish in inches of water are bonefish. There are several kinds of fish that often appear at first to be bonefish, sometimes taking even an experienced guide by surprise. For example, a barracuda. A barracuda weighing around five or six pounds may look a lot like a bonefish—they are long, slender, and silvery with a greenish back. What is more, barracuda are fun to catch. Whereas bonefish are famous for their long runs when hooked, running a hundred yards or more, barracuda jump right out of the water. To some fishermen a barracuda is even more fun to catch. A small tarpon can also give the initial impression of being a bonefish. Some anglers prefer catching a tarpon to a bonefish; they, like barracuda, are known for their spectacular jumping out of the water. There are small sharks—like the bonnet shark—that sometimes look like bonefish. They too run several yards when first hooked, making an inexperienced angler think (at first) it is a bonefish.

Bonefish, unless they show their tails in inches of water when feeding for crustaceans on the bottom, are extremely hard to see. To the angler who wants only a bonefish—and not the barracuda or shark—the challenge is terrific. But catching a bonefish is a delight that—to me at least—exceeds all other kinds of fishing. There are three stages: (1) finding the bonefish—not easy; (2) getting the bonefish to take the bait—always a challenge that requires almost perfect casting; and (3) landing the fish once it is hooked. An eight pound bonefish takes about ten minutes to bring to the net. As soon as the bonefish realizes he has been hooked, he takes off like a torpedo in the water, racing some forty miles per hour. But when he is finally brought to the net, the sense of reward is ultimate fun for the avid bonefisherman. I have caught hundreds and hundreds and never got over the thrill.

But the joy that exceeds all earthly pleasures is the joy of the true Holy Spirit. There is nothing that can rival or match the joy of the Holy Spirit. Joy is one of the fruits of the Spirit (Gal. 5:22). One should pause and realize that the joy of the Holy Spirit is *His own joy*. It is not a joy that puts your emotions on a high; it is the very joy of the Spirit Himself—it is what He feels in Himself *all the time*. So when this fruit is manifested in us, it comes with an elation and a peace that no work of the flesh can come close to assimilating. However, to the person who has come short of the joy of the Spirit, it is possible that one accepts less than the real. Why would one accept less than the real? It is possibly because they give up, possibly because the counterfeit is easier to find. It takes no effort to give in to the works of the flesh.

I'd like to share one last thing about bonefish which has often reminded me of the Holy Spirit. Apart from the fact that fishing writers have for years referred to bonefish as the "gray ghost" of shallow waters, bonefish are a lot like the Holy Spirit. They are very, very sensitive. You have to be very careful and quiet when approaching a bonefish. Make the slightest noise and the bonefish vanishes. As grieving the Spirit is easy to do, scaring a bonefish is easy to do. The greatest challenge in bonefishing is to see him before he sees you. To do this you must avoid scaring him by the slightest noise.

This is where the dove comes in. As we shall see, Jesus depicted the Holy Spirit as a dove. Why? I suppose it is because the dove by nature is a very shy, sensitive bird. Do forgive me for repeating a story that I first told in *Sensitivity of the Spirit*. It is too good to leave out, even if you read my book *Sensitivity of the Spirit*.

A British couple were sent by their denomination to be missionaries in Israel. They were given a home in which to live near Jerusalem. A few weeks after they moved into their house, they noticed that a dove had come to live in the eave of the roof of their new home. They were thrilled, choosing to believe it was a seal of God's approval of their being in Israel. But they noticed that every time they slammed a door, the dove would fly away. Every time they would get into an argument with each other and start shouting, the dove would fly away.

One day Sandy said to Bernice, "How do you feel about the dove?"

"It's like a seal of God on our being here," she replied.

"Have you noticed that every time we slam a door, the dove flies away? Every time we get into an argument with each other and start shouting, the dove flies away?"

"Yes," she replied, "and I am so afraid the dove will fly off and never return."

"Either the dove adjusts to us or we adjust to the dove," Sandy said to Bernice.

Their effort to keep the dove in the eave of the roof of their home changed their lives. The purpose of this book is to change your life. I can testify that the teaching that lies behind this book has done more to shape and change my own life than any insight I have come across. I pray it will do this for you.

It is not hard to keep a pigeon around. They are among the most unlikeable birds in the world. Their droppings have endangered homes, bridges, and statues. Their droppings also contain fungi that are dangerous. I have seen signs in the London Underground:

DO NOT FEED THE PIGEONS, THEY ARE A NUISANCE.

Former Mayor of London Ken Livingstone did his best to get rid of all pigeons in many public places.

To keep the Dove—the Holy Spirit—around, however, is a different kind of challenge. It is the most formidable pursuit I have ever come across. It is also the most rewarding pursuit I know of. In other words, the easiest thing in the world to do is to grieve the Holy Spirit; the hardest thing in the world to do is to keep from grieving the Holy Spirit.

I wonder if many of us have at times confused a pigeon for a dove. Like my mistake at the Western Wall, the power of suggestion shapes our expectancy to such an extent that we hastily assume the Dove has come, but a more objective examination reveals the embarrassing truth.

It is an easy mistake to make.

Chapter 1

THE HOLY SPIRIT
AND THE DOVE

Then John bore witness, saying, "I saw the Spirit descending from heaven like a dove, and it remained on Him. I did not know Him, but He who sent me to baptize with water said to me, 'The One on whom you see the Spirit descending and remaining, this is He who baptizes with the Holy Spirit.' I have seen and have borne witness that He is the Son of God."

—JOHN 1:32–34

———— ◆ ————

Pigeons are unafraid of people and noise; doves are hypersensitive and afraid of people.

————

SOON AFTER WE moved to Oxford in the autumn of 1973, we were anxious to see London. We visited Buckingham Palace, Big Ben, and Trafalgar Square. Trafalgar Square became a favorite place for our son TR, then six years old. He loved the pigeons. I have a picture of TR with four pigeons on each arm and two on his head! He thought he had gone to heaven! While pigeons were eating, TR actually walked over to a pigeon and picked it up and held it. You could not do this with a dove; doves are afraid of people. I doubt whether a dove ever comes near Trafalgar Square.

The Holy Spirit is often depicted as a dove in the New Testament. But He is also depicted as wind, fire, possibly water, and also oil. Many of us cry to God that the "fire" of the Holy Spirit will fall. Oh that this might happen in our lifetime! Nothing is more needed than for the fire of Pentecost to fall on us in our day!

MY THEORY

However, I have a theory. Could it be that the more crucial need at the moment is that the *Dove* will come down on us? The Dove of the Holy Spirit came down on Jesus. And remained. I wish the Dove of the Holy Spirit would fall on us. And stay!

To put my theory slightly differently: if we become more acquainted with God's ways, the dove will consequently come down on us, and the fire falling will not be far away! Before the fire fell at Pentecost, the one hundred twenty people had time to sort out things among themselves. "They were all together in one place" (Acts 2:1). *All together* suggests they had unity. This suggests the absence of bitterness and pointing the finger. We could get it backward if we pray only for the fire to fall. If we create conditions whereby the ungrieved Spirit is at home with us, it seems to me it will be more likely for the fire to fall.

In summary: the dove first, then the fire.

If we become more acquainted with God's ways, the dove will consequently come down on us, and the fire falling will not be far away!

The four gospels—the Gospel of John and the synoptic gospels—all indicate how the Holy Spirit is depicted as a dove.

> And when Jesus was baptized, He came up imme-
> diately out of the water. And suddenly the heavens
> were opened to Him, and He saw the Spirit of God

descending on Him like a dove. And a voice came from heaven, saying, "This is My beloved Son, in whom I am well pleased."

—MATTHEW 3:16–17

Coming up out of the water, He immediately saw the heavens opened and the Spirit descending on Him like a dove. And a voice came from heaven, saying, "You are My beloved Son in whom I am well pleased."

—MARK 1:10–11

Now when all the people were baptized, and when Jesus also had been baptized and was praying, the heavens were opened, and the Holy Spirit descended in a bodily form like a dove on Him, and a voice came from heaven which said, "You are My beloved Son. In You I am well pleased."

—LUKE 3:21–22

God probably chose to depict the Holy Spirit as a dove because the turtledove is a very shy, harmless, innocent bird. Jesus implied this when He described the dove as such: "I am sending you out as sheep in the midst of wolves. Therefore be wise as serpents and harmless as doves" (Matt. 10:16). The word *harmless* comes from the Greek *akeraios*, meaning "pure or morally innocent." It describes a person who has not become corrupted. The Holy Spirit is pure like heavenly wisdom.

But the wisdom that is from above is first pure, then peaceable, gentle, open to reason, full of mercy and good fruits, without partiality, and without hypocrisy. And the fruit of righteousness is sown in peace by those who make peace.

—JAMES 3:17–18

The dove, being a very sensitive bird, is mostly afraid of people. Unlike the pigeon, which easily adjusts to noise and people, the dove cannot cope well with people nor be trained. One can train a pigeon, but it is difficult to get very close to a dove; they fly away before you get a chance. Try petting a dove! It's almost impossible. But you *can* pet a pigeon.

My previously mentioned picture of our son TR at London's Trafalgar Square was taken long before Mayor Ken Livingstone stopped the practice of people feeding pigeons there. In those days pigeons would swarm you. Sprinkle some seed on your arms and down they would come. My memories of this phenomenon convince me that pigeons are not afraid of people—unlike the shy, elusive dove. The dove is sensitive.

The Holy Spirit is depicted as being sensitive. I would say hypersensitive. When I wrote my book *Sensitivity of the Spirit*, I initially thought of titling it "The Hypersensitivity of the Spirit," but I realized people would not know what I meant by that. However, it cannot be exaggerated how sensitive the third person of the Trinity is.

This aspect of the Holy Spirit's person—or personality—was something I began to discover in my early days at Westminster Chapel. Yes, I actually discovered this by my personal experience. I will explain.

I recall so vividly the days when I first came to see how sensitive the Holy Spirit is. I had made a commitment not to grieve the Holy Spirit, but I soon came to learn by experience that the slightest thing *would* grieve Him: if I answered someone curtly over the phone—especially when trying to make a plane reservation; or when Louise would annoy me and I would retort; or if I shouted at our children. It seemed that the Holy Spirit gave me no slack. The "least" thing seemed to grieve Him.

How did I know? The next time I tried to pray or read my Bible—not to mention prepare a sermon—I felt utterly on my own. When He was grieved, I would lose presence of mind and the ability to think clearly. I remember how in those days I thought, "This is not fair! Who can help but grieve the Holy Spirit?" I became frustrated with the Holy Spirit Himself!

Perhaps this is not unlike the way David initially felt when trying to move the ark of the covenant into Jerusalem. This was a noble, holy, and God-honoring thing to do. You would have thought that God would honor David and bless him for this totally spiritual decision. But when the oxen carrying the ark came to a certain place, they stumbled. A man named Uzzah did what surely seemed to be a reasonable thing to do: he took hold of the ark to steady it lest it fall to the ground. But what he did was wrong. "The LORD became angry against Uzzah, and God struck him down on the spot for his irreverence" (2 Sam. 6:6–7). Uzzah was struck dead right on the spot. As for David, his reaction was anger "because of the outburst of the LORD against Uzzah" (v. 8).

That was much the way I felt in my early days at Westminster Chapel (late 1970s and early '80s), trying so hard not to grieve the Spirit. It was surely a good vow to make, but I did not win any points from God. He would not bend the rules for me. The moment I would do certain things—like lose my temper—I began to sense the dove flying away. It could happen at any moment: driving behind a slow car on the motorway; showing impatience when a person ahead of me in a supermarket spent what seemed like hours counting their change; allowing jealousy to make me speak negatively against someone; saying something complimentary about myself to impress someone. These things resulted almost immediately in a loss of the *sense* of God's presence. Instead of God rewarding me for trying to walk closer to God and not grieve His Spirit, the efforts seemed to get even more difficult.

As for David, he was angry but he soon cooled off. His fear of the Lord returned and he asked, "How can the ark of the LORD come to me?" (v. 9). David did not abandon his resolve. He made moving the ark into Jerusalem a priority.

By climbing down and cooling off, he discovered that they had not gone about things in the prescribed way (1 Chron. 15:13). The ark was never to be touched but carried on long poles that went through rings on the ark. That way no human touched it. So David bowed to Scripture and eventually succeeded in moving the ark into Jerusalem. "The Levites lifted up the ark of God just as Moses commanded, with the poles on their shoulders, according to the word of the LORD" (1 Chron. 15:15).

God would not bend the rules for David. He will not bend the rules for you and me. As Sandy said to Bernice (read their story in my introduction), "Either the dove adjusts to us or we adjust to the dove."

TWO NOTABLE THINGS THE NEW TESTAMENT SAYS ABOUT THE HOLY SPIRIT

1. He can be grieved.

"And do not grieve the Holy Spirit of God, in whom you are sealed for the day of redemption" (Eph. 4:30). The word *grieved* comes from a word that means to get your feelings hurt. The Holy Spirit has feelings. As I said, He is very sensitive.

When we normally speak of someone being very sensitive it is probably not a compliment. We say this when we must walk on eggshells around someone, knowing the slightest misstatement will offend them. But like it or not, this is the way the Holy Spirit is! I can tell you—categorically—the Holy Spirit is hypersensitive. I have preached all around the globe that the easiest thing in the world to do is to grieve the Holy Spirit. The things that grieve Him seem as innocent as Uzzah attempting to steady the ark lest it fall on the ground.

We grieve the Spirit mostly by a wrong attitude—chiefly, bitterness. As soon as Paul said not to grieve the Holy Spirit of God, he followed with these words: "Let all bitterness, wrath, anger, outbursts, and blasphemies, with all malice, be taken away from you. And be kind one to another, tenderhearted, forgiving one another, just as God in Christ also forgave you" (Eph. 4:31–32).

Grieving the Spirit, then, is mostly internal. It is in our hearts: hateful thoughts, evil desires or wishes. Most of what grieves the Holy Spirit is an unforgiving spirit that manifests itself in bitterness, which is inward anger.

2. He can be quenched.

"Do not quench the Spirit" (1 Thess. 5:19). What is the difference between *grieving* the Spirit and *quenching* Him? It pertains to what is internal and what is external. The difference between grieving the Spirit and quenching the Spirit partly comes to this: we grieve Him when *inwardly* we lose control and we lose the presence of His mind; we quench the Spirit when He is at work *outwardly* and we object to His ways. It may happen when you are critical of the way He chooses to work. You quench the Spirit when you speak ill of what is happening. You may also quench the Spirit when you mislead another person regarding what God may be doing.

We learn from Jonathan Edwards that the task of every generation is to discover in which direction the Sovereign Redeemer is moving, then move in that direction. Unfortunately, what often happens instead is that we quench the Spirit when we object to the way God chooses to show up. It happens today, and it happened in Edwards's time. People criticized the manifestations of the Spirit in the Great Awakening (1735–1750)—people "swooning" (falling down), laughing, shouting, and sometimes barking like dogs! Likewise, people have objected to some of the manifestations in every movement, outpouring, and revival since that time. This can be quenching the Spirit.

What is the difference between grieving the
Spirit and quenching Him? It pertains to
what is internal and what is external.

As I said in my book *Holy Fire*, and will repeat below, the speculative teaching called Cessationism (that God chose to "cease" the miraculous working of the Spirit many years ago) also quenches the Holy Spirit. It rules out the possibility of manifestations today before the Spirit gets a chance to show up!

During the Welsh Revival (1904–1905) a British couple serving as missionaries in India heard that revival had broken out in Wales. They immediately made plans to get to Britain as soon as possible. They arrived at Southampton and headed for London. They ran into old friends who asked, "Whatever are you doing back in London?" They replied that they were on their way to Wales in order to see the great revival that had broken out there. Their friends intervened and said to them, "Oh, don't bother; it is not revival at all, it is Welsh emotionalism." The British missionaries turned around and went back to India. Their old friends had quenched the Holy Spirit, and sadly it stopped them from seeing a true work of God. That is a way one may quench the Spirit.

Thankfully not everyone shared their perspective of the revival. Mrs. Martyn Lloyd-Jones told me about when she was six years old and living in London, her father put her on a train from London to Wales in order that she might see the revival for herself. People criticized her dad for taking her out of school and putting her on a train for Wales. His reply: "She can always go to school. She may never see revival again." What a wise father! Mrs. Lloyd-Jones used to share with me her feelings when sitting in those meetings as a six-year-old girl. She was blessed with that experience because her father, rather than quenching the Spirit, honored the Spirit.

I was named after my father's favorite preacher, Dr. R. T. Williams, who was general superintendent of the Church of the Nazarene. He gave this advice to young ministers: "Honor the blood and honor the Holy Ghost." That's pretty good advice, if you ask me! Honoring the blood means never taking for granted the price Jesus paid on Calvary's cross. Honoring the Holy Spirit is respecting His very person and presence.

In my early days as a Nazarene, when visiting evangelists would give the altar call they would urge the congregation not to quench the Spirit. They may have gone to extremes—even fearing a baby crying during the altar call—in being too careful. And yet the point was driven home to me.

John the Baptist knew that Jesus was the true Messiah because he had been told to watch for the dove descending on a person "and remaining." The fact of the dove descending is what people mostly notice. How many notice the word *remain*—twice in John 1:32–33. The Holy Spirit came upon Jesus and *stayed there.* The Spirit "remained" on Him, never leaving Jesus.

My Personal Frustration

I know what it is for the Holy Spirit to fall on me—sometimes in my quiet time, sometimes at church, sometimes driving in my car. It is my experience that He often comes without notice, without any warning. This gives one an expectancy every day! "The wind blows where it wishes, and you hear its sound, but you do not know where it comes from or where it goes," said Jesus when teaching the sovereignty of the Spirit to Nicodemus (John 3:8).

But here's my problem. I have found invariably (sadly) that when the Spirit comes down, He does not *remain.* While this blessing lasts it is wonderful. Indescribable. The peace truly passes understanding. The awareness of how *real* He is. I think to myself, or pray: "Lord, please don't leave. Don't go. Don't let there be any interruption." But hours later, as life goes on, I find myself "back to normal"—not feeling so aware of His presence and peace.

Why? What happened? First, it is possible I did nothing wrong. After all, the Holy Spirit is sovereign. And yet all He does is to mirror the sovereignty of God. God said to Moses, "I will have mercy on whom I have mercy, and I will have compassion on whom I have compassion" (Rom. 9:15). And yet there is more: the Holy Spirit only does what the Father directs Him to do. Jesus Himself was not His "own man." He said so. "The Son can do nothing of Himself, but what He sees the Father do. For whatever He does, likewise the Son does" (John 5:19). Jesus also said that the Holy Spirit does not "speak on His own authority. But He will speak whatever He hears" (John 16:13). This shows in what sense the Son and the Holy Spirit are alike. Neither Jesus nor the Holy Spirit acted on their own; all they would do mirrored the sovereign will of the Father.

This means that as the Holy Spirit may descend upon us unexpectedly and without notice, so likewise He may lift His manifest presence without notice. It does not mean we have done anything wrong. It does not necessarily mean we have grieved Him.

That said, I know from personal experience that sometimes it *is* my impatience and unguarded comments that grieve the Holy Spirit.

WHAT HAPPENS WHEN WE GRIEVE THE HOLY SPIRIT?

There are two further things to be said about grieving the Spirit. The first is, grieving the Holy Spirit does not forfeit our salvation. Paul said, "Do not grieve the Holy Spirit of God, in whom you are sealed for the day of redemption" (Eph. 4:30). Nothing could be clearer than that! The Holy Spirit *seals* us for the day of redemption. Our redemption—salvation—cannot be forfeited. In other words, my bitterness, anger, losing my temper, or withholding forgiveness does not put my salvation in jeopardy. If that is true, what happens, then, when I grieve the Spirit? Answer: I lose the *sense* of His manifest presence. I do not lose the Holy Spirit. When He comes, He comes to stay! He will abide with us "forever," said Jesus (John 14:16). But His *manifest presence*—the sweet peace, presence of mind, knowledge that I am pleasing Him, the clear thinking and sense of authority and power—may diminish. That is what happens.

So when the Spirit comes down on me by unveiling His manifest presence, it is for a season. It could be minutes, it could be hours, or it could be days. The first time the manifest presence of the Holy Spirit came on me, it lasted for about ten months. And then—I will never forget it as long as I live—this incredible peace and rest simply left. I can tell you what happened. I lost my temper with someone and then—suddenly—this powerful sense of God diminished.

So when the Dove came down on Jesus, He remained. He stayed. Jesus never ever grieved or quenched the Holy Spirit. When the Dove of the Holy Spirit came on Jesus, I think the Spirit said, "I like it here. I am at home here. I am going to stay right here." The Dove remained on Jesus. There was nothing in the heart and mind of Jesus that made the Holy Spirit uncomfortable. There was not a shred of bitterness in Jesus; no anger or desire to get even. The greatest freedom is having nothing to prove, says my friend Pete Cantrell; Jesus had nothing to prove. There was not a trace of unforgiveness in Jesus, no hint of holding a grudge.

If we are going to manifest Christlikeness, it means that we will be like Jesus in the manner I have just described. There will be no grudges seething inside of us. No plans for revenge. No efforts to prove ourselves. No intentions of getting even. As Jesus prayed for His enemies at the Cross—"Father, forgive them, for they know not what they do" (Luke 23:34)—so must we likewise pray for our enemies. And when we pray for our enemies, we do not avoid our responsibility by saying, "Lord, I commit them to You." No. We actually pray for God to *bless* our enemies (Luke 6:27–28). This kind of demeanor is what makes the Holy Spirit perfectly at home with us. This is why the Dove was utterly at home with Jesus.

In a word: the Dove felt completely and totally at home when He descended on Jesus. And there He remained.

The consciousness of the Dove never left Jesus—that is,

until Good Friday between noon and 3:00 p.m. For those three hours the Shekinah glory—the dark cloud—enveloped the land (Matt. 27:45), and Jesus cried out, "My God, My God, why have You forsaken Me?" (Mark 15:34). The darkness that covered the land was not an eclipse of the sun but the presence of God. It was a seal on the atonement. God promised to "appear in the cloud on the mercy seat" on the Day of Atonement (Lev. 16:2). It was a "dark cloud," God said to Solomon (2 Chron. 6:1). That darkness was God's seal upon the shed blood of Jesus. Thus the only time Jesus lost the sense of the presence of God with Him was the moment when "God made Him who knew no sin to be sin for us, that we might become the righteousness of God in Him" (2 Cor. 5:21).

In other words, the Holy Spirit came down on Jesus and "remained." Throughout His three-year ministry that led up to the Cross, the Dove—the ungrieved Holy Spirit—remained on Jesus. What is more: Jesus had the Holy Spirit "without measure" (John 3:34). You and I, though it may be said we are "filled" with the Holy Spirit, in fact only have a "measure" or "limit" of faith (Rom. 12:3). Jesus alone had a perfect faith. This is because He had the Holy Spirit—His manifest presence—without measure. He lost that only for some two or three hours. It was the only time He addressed His father as "God." All other times He addressed Him as Father. Thus when this bleak sense of God leaving Jesus ended, the fellowship was restored moments before His death. He cried out, "It is finished" (John 19:30), then looked into His Father's face and said with a loud voice, "Father, into Your hands I commit My spirit" (Luke 23:46).

The way to become more and more like Jesus in our demeanor and conduct is to remember that the Dove was at home with Jesus. And why? It was because Jesus was full of peace and forgiveness; a man devoid of bitterness.

Chapter 2

THE DOVE'S WAYS

He will guide you into all truth. For He will not speak on His own authority. But He will speak whatever He hears.

—JOHN 16:13

———— ◆ ————

Pigeons are aggressive. Doves are not aggressive.

————

I SO WANTED TO meet Nelson Mandela. Almost more than any pursuit in my life, I persevered *so* diligently to meet that great man. I met several people who knew him. A number of people assured me that they would arrange for me to meet Nelson Mandela. A South African general phoned me from Paris, saying, "I hear you want to meet Nelson Mandela." He promised to make it happen. I never heard from him again. I wrote letters to South Africa. When I went to South Africa, I managed to meet Mandela's right hand man in the president's office. I was almost there—right outside his door. But everything fell through. I cannot recall any equivalent effort in my life to which I devoted so much energy as trying to meet that man. It seemed so right. It even appeared so providential.

On the day I hoped to meet him—on a plane from Johannesburg to Cape Town—my Bible reading included this verse: "But are you seeking great things for yourself? Do not seek them" (Jer. 45:5). I was smitten. That did it. I knew right then in

my heart that God was saying "No" to my pursuit. My aggres-
siveness used to work when I sold life insurance. My aggres-
siveness worked when I was a door-to-door vacuum cleaner
salesman. But now I was in a different situation; I needed the
Holy Spirit to make this happen. My pigeon-like behavior did
not work when it came to meeting Nelson Mandela.

When we want the Holy Spirit to work on our behalf, we
have to give up our old ways. It means playing by a different set
of rules. The Holy Spirit will not bend the rules for any of us.

In this chapter I want to lay the theological groundwork
for a solid, sound, and straightforward New Testament
teaching on the Holy Spirit. But first let's look a little more
closely at this iconic symbol.

THE SYMBOL OF THE DOVE

From ancient times—long before it was seen as a symbol of
the Holy Spirit in the New Testament—the dove has been
regarded as a symbol of peace. Doves were often singled out
in paganism. The dove was the sacred animal of Aphrodite
and Venus, the goddesses of love and friendship. In 1949
Pablo Picasso's lithograph *La Columbe*, a traditional picture
of a pigeon (funnily enough), was chosen as the emblem for
the World Peace Congress in Paris. A dove became a symbol
of the peace movement. In American politics there was a
time when one was identified either as a dove (for peace not
war) or a hawk (symbolizing that one was pro-war).

Noah released a dove after the Flood in order to find land.
It came back carrying an olive branch in its beak (Gen. 8:11).
This told Noah that somewhere there was land. Some theolo-
gians relate the dove in Song of Songs 2:12 to the Holy Spirit:
"The flowers appear on the earth; the time of singing has
come, and the voice of the turtledove is heard in our land."
The ancient Jewish scholar Philo saw the dove as a symbol of
the *logos* (word), the *nous* (mind), or *sophia* (wisdom).

It is probably the turtledove to which the Bible mainly

refers, although that in itself would not be of ultimate importance. *Peristera* is the Greek word for dove, *trygon* for turtledove; but *peristera* could also refer to a turtledove.

As we have seen, pigeons and doves both belong to the same order of birds, namely, the Columbiformes, and yet the Bible makes a distinction between pigeons and doves (Lev. 12:8). The focus of this book is to understand the authentic Holy Spirit, symbolized by a dove, and see the difference between it and a pigeon.

Why raise the question, "Is it the Dove or is it 'Pigeon Religion'?" As I have shared, in the natural, some may think they are seeing a dove when it is really a pigeon. In the spiritual, some may think they are witnessing the anointing of the Holy Spirit when it is in fact pigeon religion.

Some may think the Holy Spirit has come down, when it isn't the Holy Spirit after all. Therefore we are obliged to be sure that we recognize not only the Dove but also the counterfeit! As the bonefisherman needs to recognize the difference between a bonefish and a barracuda, so do we all need to discern the authentic Holy Spirit from pigeon religion.

At Jesus's baptism "the heavens were opened" (Matt. 3:16). By Matthew's and Mark's accounts it would seem that Jesus Himself saw the Spirit descending like a dove. But John's Gospel states that John the Baptist saw the dove come down (John 1:32). We may conclude that both John and Jesus saw the dove. Did bystanders see it too? You tell me. What also stands out was the voice from heaven: "This is My beloved Son, in whom I am well pleased" (Matt. 3:17).

In the natural, some may think they are seeing a dove when it is really a pigeon. In the spiritual, some may think they are witnessing the anointing of the Holy Spirit when it is in fact pigeon religion.

What was the importance of the dove? We are told the Spirit descended "like a dove." This is obviously what John saw. But why should the dove be present for Jesus's baptism? My answer: it shows the Trinitarian witness to His baptism. The voice from heaven was God the Father; the dove represented the Holy Spirit. It shows the importance of Jesus's baptism.

But why was Jesus baptized? First, He affirmed John the Baptist. John the Baptist was the voice crying in the wilderness, fulfilling Isaiah's prophecy (Matt. 3:3; Isa. 40:3). John raised the ire of the Jews in Jerusalem. People came all the way from Jerusalem to hear John. Jesus endorsed John by asking to be baptized by him.

Second, Jesus fulfilled "all righteousness" by being baptized (Matt. 3:15)—*for us*. John's baptism was a baptism of repentance; but Jesus did not need to repent. So why was He baptized? To demonstrate that He did *everything* required of us in order to be saved. He kept the Law for us (Matt. 5:17), and was therefore even baptized for us. In doing so, not only did Jesus affirm John's ministry; the Holy Spirit also affirmed Jesus's baptism.

All four Gospels state that the dove witnessed Jesus's baptism. This shows how important the event was. That said, it is far more important to recognize the real than it is to become an expert when it comes to the counterfeit.

Many years ago I knew of a young man who applied for a job at a bank in his hometown. He got the job and soon became very ambitious. His goal was to impress the bank's president, hoping it would lead to rapid promotions. He came up with the idea of becoming an expert in counterfeit money. He became obsessed with counterfeit money. He bought books on the subject. He wanted to learn how to instantly recognize the counterfeit. The bank's president caught wind of the young man's aim and called him into his office. While commending him for his ambition, the elderly president of the bank gave this advice: "Young man, if you are wanting to be able to recognize counterfeit money, start by becoming an expert in what is *real*. Learn the ring and feel of a silver dollar, become an expert in discovering a true twenty dollar bill and a genuine hundred dollar bill, and you will have no difficulty in spotting the counterfeit when it comes."

I therefore propose to outline what is absolutely true about the Holy Spirit, the third person of the Trinity, before we move on. If you want more detail, please see my book *Forty Days With the Holy Spirit*. I will summarize what I believe to be the essential things to be said about Him.

SIXTEEN ESSENTIAL TRUTHS ABOUT THE HOLY SPIRIT

1. The Holy Spirit is God.

This is the first and most important thing. The Holy Spirit is God as the Father is God and Jesus is God. This means that He will faithfully represent and reflect the God of the Bible. The Holy Spirit is never an "it." The Holy Spirit is always *He*. He is a person—equally as Jesus is a person and God the Father is a person. Not an influence or mood but a person. He is distinct from the Father and the Son and yet in total and complete unity with the Father and the Son. Do you thoroughly grasp this? Probably not. Who can? And yet you embrace it because this is what Scripture teaches. Don't try to figure Him out. Just listen to Him. Follow Him. It is the only way you know you will not be deceived. It is because you are following *God*.

2. The Holy Spirit is the Spirit of truth.

Jesus called Him this twice (John 14:17; 16:13). That is the way Jesus described the coming Counselor (John 14:16–17). As God Himself cannot lie (Heb. 6:18; Titus 1:2), so too is it impossible for the Holy Spirit to lie. The Holy Spirit is incapable of error, and one way you can know for sure you have the true Holy Spirit leading and guiding you is that you come into the *truth*. By that I mean you want preeminently to uphold *truth*; you love the *truth* and follow *truth* no matter the cost you may pay. The Bible says that strong and powerful delusion to believe a lie will come to those who do not have a love for the truth and will not accept the truth (2 Thess. 2:11–12). Jesus Christ is the way, the *truth,* and the life (John 14:6). All who love the truth no matter the stigma can be assured they will not embrace lies and be deceived.

3. The Holy Spirit convicts the world of sin, righteousness, and judgment (John 16:8).

This is His initial work. As we will see later, pigeon religion will not convict of sin. Pigeon religion will embrace the world without any need for repentance or change of lifestyle. Dove religion *begins* with convicting of sin when it comes to reaching the unconverted. Jesus died on the cross for our *sins.* Not to make us happy, but to save us from the wrath to come (1 Thess. 1:10). "I'm sorry for my sins" should be a part of any prayer to God when we come to God for the first time. If one is *not* sorry for his or her sins, it smacks of being affected by "another Jesus, whom we have not preached," or "another spirit," or "another gospel" (2 Cor. 11:4).

4. The Holy Spirit will affirm the God of the Old Testament.

On the Day of Pentecost, Peter preached with the same power that had enabled the one hundred twenty disciples to speak in other tongues. A fascinating study of the Greek shows that the same word is used when describing the "utterance" that enabled one hundred twenty people to speak in other languages (Acts 2:4, ESV) and the "address" Peter gave in his own language (Acts 2:14, ESV). Immediately Peter affirmed the Old Testament, quoting the promise of Joel 2:28. (See Acts 2:17.) Dove religion will not apologize for the God of the Old Testament. Jesus never apologized for the God of the Old Testament—His Father. Are you ashamed of the God of the Old Testament? If so, I must say to you—with respect—you are not upholding Dove religion. After all, the Holy Spirit wrote the Old Testament (2 Tim. 3:16; 2 Pet. 1:21).

5. The Holy Spirit is the God of purpose.

Speaking at the highest possible level of anointing, Peter reminded his hearers on the Day of Pentecost that the death of Jesus Christ was no accident. Many of Jesus's followers were bewildered: *How could this happen? How could the man who raised Lazarus from the dead have allowed Himself to be crucified?* Answer: Jesus "was handed over to you by the ordained counsel and foreknowledge of God" (Acts 2:23). Yes, when they crucified Jesus they did what God "had foreordained to be done" (Acts 4:28). In a word: predestination was behind Jesus's death. God declares the end from the beginning (Isa. 46:10). Anything less than this is pigeon religion.

6. The Holy Spirit makes Jesus as real as He had been in the flesh.

Jesus told the disciples, "In a little while you will not see Me; and then after a little while you will see Me" (John 16:19). This puzzled the disciples. But when the Spirit came down on them at Pentecost, the puzzle was solved. So *real* was Jesus to Peter that he quoted Psalm 16:8—"I have set the LORD always before me"—except that Peter quoted it, "I foresaw the Lord always before me" (Acts 2:25). Yes, Peter saw Jesus by the Spirit as he preached. Whereas the disciples thought they had lost Jesus when He ascended to the right hand of the Father, in truth they got Him back by the immediate and direct witness and revelation of the Holy Spirit.

7. The Holy Spirit achieves His aim through preaching.

Whereas at the beginning of Peter's sermon in Acts chapter 2 people made fun of the disciples, no one was laughing when he finished. They had one question: "What shall we do?" This is called "effectual calling." The great Charles Spurgeon loved to quote Psalm 110:3 from the King James Version: "Thy people shall be willing in the day of thy power." The same was true in the conversion of Saul of Tarsus. He was fighting hard against "the pricks" (Acts

26:14, KJV). But he succumbed to the power of the Spirit and cried out, "What shall I do, Lord?" (Acts 22:10). God's Word tells us that "those whom He called, He also justified" (Rom. 8:30). It is through the "foolishness of preaching" that God saves those who believe (1 Cor. 1:21).

8. The Holy Spirit vindicates Jesus's resurrection through signs and wonders.

A forty-year-old man crippled from birth was given instant healing. This should not surprise us, said Peter, since God raised Jesus from the dead. "And His name, by faith in His name, has made this man strong, whom you see and know. And faith which comes through Him has given him perfect health in your presence" (Acts 3:16). Indeed, "many signs and wonders were performed among the people by the hands of the apostles" (Acts 5:12). People brought the sick into the streets and laid them on beds and mats so that at least Peter's shadow might fall on some of them as he passed by (Acts 5:15). There is no reason whatever that these signs and wonders cannot be repeated in our day. Jesus Christ is the same yesterday, today, and forever (Heb. 13:8). So too the Holy Spirit is the same yesterday, today, and forever!

9. The Holy Spirit gives immediate and direct guidance.

Philip was told to head out toward a certain road—one from Jerusalem to Gaza. He did not know why. But when he saw an important Ethiopian official sitting in a chariot, "the Spirit said to Philip, 'Go to this chariot and stay with it'" (Acts 8:29). By that time Philip knew why he was led as he was. The result was that this Ethiopian was converted and immediately baptized (Acts 8:35–38). One of the fringe benefits of having the Holy Spirit is that He shows us things— where to go, when to go, and if necessary, when we've got it right and when we've got it wrong: "And if you think differently in any way, God will reveal even this to you" (Phil. 3:15).

10. The Holy Spirit leads to the truth.

"But when the Spirit of truth comes, He will guide you into all truth" (John 16:13). His word is "truth" (John 17:17). The Holy Spirit will not lead to error, heresy (false doctrine), or whatever is contrary to Scripture. As it is impossible for God to lie, so it is impossible for the Holy Spirit to mislead us, including theologically. The Spirit of truth will not deceive us. He who wrote Holy Scripture will never lead us to embrace what is not biblical. He will help us *handle* correctly the "word of truth" (2 Tim. 2:15). Therefore, if we are led of the Holy Spirit, we will not merely say what is "true," we will utter *truth* when speaking in God's name.

11. The Holy Spirit witnesses to what are facts.

Jesus died on a cross. That is a fact. Jesus was raised from the dead. That is a fact. On one occasion, over five hundred saw Jesus after He was raised from the dead (1 Cor. 15:6). That is a fact. Therefore, when Peter and the apostles said to the Sanhedrin that Jesus not only died and rose from the dead but was exalted to the right hand of God, they were stating facts. That is what was meant by their words, "we are His witnesses to these words" (Acts 5:32). They were witnessing to *facts*. But they added: "So is the Holy Spirit." What did that mean? It meant the Holy Spirit did not merely see all these things happening but that He made this inescapably clear to the apostles—by His immediate and direct testimony. So if the *Holy Spirit* indicated that something happened, it happened. It was as though they might say, "We would believe what the Holy Spirit said even if we had not seen the risen Jesus for ourselves." That is how real, reliable, and powerful the testimony of the Spirit is!

12. The Holy Spirit affirmed Gentiles being converted without their being circumcised.

As the Spirit spoke directly to Philip, He said to Peter, who had been praying, "Three men are looking for you. So rise and go down, and go with them, doubting nothing. For I have sent them" (Acts 10:19–20). As a result, Peter went to the house of Cornelius, a Gentile, and preached to him and those with him. As Peter spoke, the Holy Spirit fell on all who heard the message. How did they know it was the Holy Spirit? They were "speaking in other tongues and magnifying God" (Acts 10:44–46). You can be sure it was the speaking in tongues that convinced them of the presence of the Holy Spirit on them. Likewise, when Paul laid hands on the Ephesians, they spoke in tongues (Acts 19:6). In both cases it was speaking in tongues that provided the undoubted proof that the Holy Spirit had fallen on them.

13. The Holy Spirit intercedes for us.

Whereas Jesus our great High Priest intercedes for us at the Father's right hand (Heb. 4:14–16), Paul tells us that the Holy Spirit does this too. Paul admitted that he did not always know how to pray or what to pray for. Sometimes a burden came on him and the best he could do was to *groan*. The King James Version says the Spirit intercedes for us with "groanings which cannot be uttered" (Rom. 8:26). The New International Version says: "wordless groans." The English Standard Version and Modern English Version: "groanings too deep for words." Could this be Paul praying in tongues? Yes. This is one of the great benefits of praying in the Spirit; you don't know what you are saying—strange as this may be to some—but one thing is for certain: the Spirit intercedes in accordance with God's will. It is at least one time you know when you are praying in the will of God. It is also when Satan for certain does not know what you are praying!

14. The Holy Spirit regards us as His temple.

This is one of the most thrilling yet sobering of all the truths concerning the Spirit and us. First, how thrilling to know that the Holy Spirit dwells in us. He never leaves us. He is always there. We are His. "Your body is a temple of the Holy Spirit" (1 Cor. 6:19). Not only that; we are "bought with a price" (v. 20)—namely, Christ's blood. That means we are not our own. We are His. But the sobering part of this truth is that we are to honor God with our bodies. Hence any abuse of our bodies—e.g., sexual activity outside of marriage—displeases God. "He who commits sexual immorality sins against his own body" (v. 18). The consequence could be extreme disciplining from God. It is a warning that God wants sexual purity for all His own.

15. The Holy Spirit manifests Himself through various gifts.

First Corinthians 12:8–10 gives a list of nine gifts. More gifts are added in 1 Corinthians 12:28–30. A different kind of list—sometimes called motivational gifts—is found in Romans 12:6–8. We are exhorted to desire earnestly the "higher," "best," or "greater" gifts (1 Cor. 12:31, ESV, KJV, NIV). This shows that some gifts are more important than others. It also shows that although the gifts are sovereignly bestowed according to God's will (1 Cor. 12:11), we should nonetheless seek those we desire. It certainly means asking God to give them. And yet, paradoxically, "the gifts and calling of God are irrevocable" (Rom. 11:29). This shows that our worthiness will not move God to grant them, neither does our unworthiness cause one to lose them. This is scary. The gifts of the Spirit are not an indication of our spirituality.

16. The Holy Spirit manifests Himself through various fruits.

"But the fruit of the Spirit is love, joy, peace, patience, gentleness, goodness, faith, meekness, and self-control" (Gal. 5:22–23). Whereas the gifts of the Spirit do not show how spiritual or obedient one is, the fruit of the Holy Spirit certainly indicates whether we are obedient. The gifts are permanent and require no measure of obedience to keep them. The fruit of the Spirit, however, is manifested in proportion to our walking in the light—in obedience to the will of Christ. The works of the flesh are manifested in "adultery, sexual immorality, impurity, lewdness, idolatry, sorcery, hatred, strife, jealousy, rage, selfishness, dissensions, heresies, envy, murders, drunkenness, carousing, and the like" (Gal. 5:19–21)—showing no self-control. These things grieve the Holy Spirit. The fruit flows out of obedience to the Word of God, causing the manifestations of pigeon religion to be less likely.

Chapter 3

LEARNING THE HOLY SPIRIT'S WAYS

Therefore, as the Holy Spirit says: "Today, if you hear His voice, do not harden your hearts as in the rebellion, on the day of temptation in the wilderness, where your fathers tested Me and tried Me and saw My works for forty years. Therefore I was angry with that generation, and said, 'They always go astray in their heart, and they have not known My ways.' So I swore in My wrath, 'They shall not enter My rest.'"
—HEBREWS 3:7–11

———— ❖ ————

Pigeons are belligerent. Doves are peaceful.

————

I WAS PREACHING IN Florence, Alabama, a few years ago. Just before I walked into the pulpit, the young pastor suddenly asked, "What has a veteran like you got to say to a young whippersnapper like me?" I had to think for a moment. Then I said to him, "Find out what grieves the Holy Spirit and don't do that."

I think that is safe advice for anyone.

You may not particularly like the Holy Spirit's ways. But He is the only Holy Spirit you have! So, as my friend Jack Taylor would say, "Get over it."

Learning God's ways, therefore, comes down basically to two things: (1) find out what grieves Him—and avoid this;

and (2) find out what pleases Him—and do whatever it takes to accomplish this. The degree to which we please the Lord will be the degree to which the Dove comes down and remains with us.

God lamented of ancient Israel, "They have not known My *ways*" (Heb. 3:10, emphasis added). God was both angry and sad. I sense the tear in God's voice in saying, "They have not known My ways"—the very thing God wanted of them.

The ancient Israelites had plenty of opportunities to learn God's ways. They witnessed the ten plagues on Egypt during the days that a recalcitrant Pharaoh would not let God's people go free. Then came Passover—when God killed the firstborn of all in Egypt. Then the crossing of the Red Sea on dry land. The manna. The command not to move unless the pillar of fire by day and cloud by night moved first. The ancient Israelites experienced firsthand what God did. If these things did not teach them God's ways, I don't know what could!

> *The degree to which we please the Lord will be the degree to which the Dove comes down and remains with us.*

But God said of them, "They have not known My ways."

This lets us know that God *wants* us to know His ways. I am moved to think that God cares so much about me that He wants me to know His ways.

I was flying from New York to Miami about twelve years ago when I came across a verse in my daily Bible reading. I had read this verse hundreds of times before, but for some reason it shook me rigid that day. It was when Moses was given *carte blanche* from God to ask whatever he wanted. Moses replied: "If I have found favor in Your sight, show me now Your *way*" (Exod. 33:13, emphasis added). I was convicted like I had not been convicted in years. I had to ask myself, What if God gave me *carte blanche*? What would I have asked for? I knew exactly what I had been asking for—and it wasn't what Moses wanted. This is what shamed me. It showed me that Moses's devotion to God was so much greater and higher and deeper than mine. It showed me why Moses was the greatest man in the Old Testament, why he was the greatest leader of men in human history. All he wanted was to know God's *ways*. He could have asked for more power and authority. He could have asked for vengeance upon his stubborn following. He could have asked for any number of things—here was his chance! He wanted one thing: to know God's ways.

"My people are destroyed for lack of knowledge," said the prophet Hosea (Hos. 4:6). They lacked knowledge of two things: God's Word and His ways.

LOGOS AND RHEMA

The word *word* is translated from either of two Greek words: *logos* and *rhema*. Since these words can sometimes be used interchangeably, we must not push the distinction too far. But generally speaking *logos* refers to Scripture, the Bible, God's Word; *rhema* may refer to a specific word—such as a prophetic word.

I have been increasingly concerned that many people in the church today seem mainly to want one thing from God—a *rhema* word. I listened to a TV preacher who began, "Don't turn that dial; I have a *rhema* word for you." Why should this be reason to stay tuned? Is it better than having an exposition of Scripture? I don't mean to be unfair, but I would have thought it shows no degree of spirituality when we only want a *rhema* word—a specific word that gives direct guidance.

If we truly want to know God's will, the best thing we can do to achieve this is to get to know *Scripture* backward and forward. It is the blessing of the Holy Spirit we want and need. He wrote Scripture—His greatest product. The best way to get to know the Bible is to get on good terms with its Author. Devour everything He wrote!

TIME IN PRAYER

How do we get to know God's *ways*? How do you get to know anybody's ways? It is by spending time with them. That is the only way to know somebody. You may think you know a famous person—actor or politician—by observing them as closely as you can: hanging on to every word, reading all you can about them. But you will never get to know *anyone* truly unless you spend time with them.

How much time do you have for God? How important is time with Him to you? How much do you pray? There will be no praying in heaven.

When I first came to Westminster Chapel, I tried to get every member to spend thirty minutes a day in prayer. You would have thought the chandeliers would fall! "Thirty minutes a day?" said one deacon. "I don't know what to say after five minutes." Martin Luther spent two hours a day in his quiet time. John Wesley spent two hours on his knees every morning before he faced the day. According to a Barna study, the average Christian spends one minute a day in prayer and the average church leader today spends around *five minutes a day* in their quiet time.[1] And you wonder why the church is powerless. Where are the John Wesleys today? Where are the Martin Luthers?

WHERE ARE THE INTERCESSORS?

Years ago I read a tract entitled *Where Are the Intercessors?* That tract has haunted me for years. Intercessory prayer is possibly the most unselfish enterprise you can be involved in. One requirement for being an intercessor: that you are self-effacing. One of the differences between pigeons and doves is that pigeons draw attention to themselves; doves do not. God is looking for those who are willing to be behind the scenes and pray for *others*.

One of the most wonderful things about Moses was that

he did not farm out the ministry of intercession to other people; he was an intercessor himself!

> Therefore He said that He would destroy them, had not Moses, His chosen one, stood before Him to intercede, to turn away His wrath from destroying them.
>
> —PSALM 106:23

On the other hand, the prophet Ezekiel lamented that an intercessor could not be found:

> I sought for a man among them who would build up the hedge and stand in the gap before Me for the land so that I would not destroy it, but I found no one.
>
> —EZEKIEL 22:30

Your willingness to be an intercessor is a challenge to your ego. Can you be an intercessor and keep quiet about it? God is looking for those who are willing to do a thankless job here below in order to be praised openly above. At Westminster Chapel we many times had two or three people interceding for me as I preached; they prayed literally underneath the large pulpit during the sermon time. The congregation did not know this was happening. Intercessory prayer is not only a thankless, self-effacing task but *hard work*.

I remember when we began an evangelism ministry at Westminster Chapel that we called the Pilot Light ministry. (I'll tell you more about how it got started a little later in this chapter.) Some years later, one of our men felt led to begin an intercessory prayer time while those in the Pilot Light ministry witnessed on the streets of London. An interesting thing happened: simultaneous with a few people interceding for the Pilot Lights, the number of people praying to receive Christ tripled if not quadrupled. Before this intercessory prayer ministry began we would occasionally have two or three people make a profession of faith on a Saturday morning. After the intercessory prayer ministry began, the numbers immediately rose to ten to fifteen who prayed to receive the Lord! Coincidence? I don't think so. Those who were willing to pray for almost two hours every Saturday were behind the scenes—standing in the gap.

Are You an Intercessor?

God wants you to know His Word *and* His ways. Both of these: His Word—Holy Scripture—and His ways, come by spending time in His presence.

The writer of the epistle to the Hebrews was concerned that his readers would repeat the ancient error of Israel and forfeit their inheritance. He was concerned that these Hebrew Christians were already "hard of hearing" (Heb. 5:11). Hardness of hearing often comes in stages. Stage one: you cup your hand over your ear when someone is speaking lest you miss what they are saying. Stage two: you get a hearing aid. Stage three: you get a stronger hearing aid. Stage four: when you are "profoundly deaf," as they would put it; when you are *stone deaf.* This is why the Holy Spirit says, "If you hear His voice" (Heb. 3:7–8). As long as you can hear God's voice, you are not stone deaf. But these Hebrew Christians were already hard of hearing—on their way to stone deafness. What happens if one is stone deaf to the Holy Spirit? They cannot be renewed "once more" to repentance (Heb. 6:4–6). By not being able to hear God speak, one is no longer changed "from glory to glory" (2 Cor. 3:18).

What Are God's Particular Ways?

First, He does not want you to have any anger in your heart. We have seen already that the chief way we grieve the Holy Spirit is by bitterness. For as soon as Paul said for us not to grieve the Holy Spirit of God, he added:

> Let all bitterness, wrath, anger, outbursts, and blasphemies, with all malice, be taken away from you. And be kind one to another, tenderhearted, forgiving one another, just as God in Christ also forgave you.
>
> —EPHESIANS 4:31–32

In the Sermon on the Mount, Jesus showed that one commits murder by *anger in the heart* (Matt. 5:21–26). This kind of thinking was not even remotely on the radar screen of the Pharisees Jesus was addressing. They felt totally satisfied that they had kept the Law of Moses as long as they did not physically murder someone. But Jesus said they were guilty of murder by anger. This is a condition of the heart.

How then does one get rid of anger in the heart? I reply: by total forgiveness. This is the only way it can be done. Jesus went on to say we should love our enemies and pray that God will bless those who persecute us. As we saw above, you don't merely say, "Lord, I commit them to You" (when you are hoping God will kill them!). You must ask God to bless them.

You may be asking, RT, isn't this a very hard thing to do? Yes, it is probably the most difficult thing in the world to do—to let your enemy completely off the hook and kiss vengeance good-bye. So, how can we do this? My answer is, see the reward that is ahead by doing it. Moses himself gave up a life of luxury in the palace of Pharaoh by looking ahead to his reward for doing so (Heb. 11:26). This proves it is not wrong to be motivated by reward. God's typical way of getting our attention is by initially appealing to our self-interest. So do not feel guilty if you are motivated by reward. That is the way God made us!

So what happens if one loves his enemies? "Then your reward will be great," said Jesus (Luke 6:35). What will the reward entail? What will it be like? I don't know. But I certainly don't want to miss it! I can categorically guarantee to every reader of this book that the reward is worth waiting for.

TOTAL FORGIVENESS

I can personally testify that the worst thing that ever happened to me turned out to be the best thing that ever happened to me. Literally. Without exaggeration I make this claim. When Louise and I faced our darkest hour years ago while at Westminster Chapel, I took the unexpected and unsolicited advice of my old friend Josef Tson: "RT, you must totally forgive them. Until you totally forgive them, you will be in chains. Release them and you will be released." I did what Josef said to do. It was the hardest thing one ever has to do. But I can now say to the whole world it was the best thing I ever did. The reward has exceeded my greatest expectations!

God will do this for you, too. He is no respecter of persons. But don't expect God to bend the rules for you. He won't. If you think for one moment that God will make an exception in your case, I can tell you, that is when you let pigeon religion replace dove religion.

This brings me to my second point about God's ways: *God wants you to close the time gap between sin and repentance.* In other words, how long does it take to convince you that you have got it wrong? Some of us are so stubborn that we say, "I will *never* admit I was wrong. I will *never* forgive them for what they did." And sadly there are those who dig in their heels and *never* forgive. What a pity that one's pride deprives him or her of God's incalculable blessing.

Don't let that be you. Don't let pigeon religion take over! The sooner you admit you got it wrong, the better. Why? So that there will be no discontinuity of anointing. Our goal should be unbroken, uninterrupted intimacy with the Holy Spirit. As soon as you see you were in the wrong, admit it and repent at once! I've seen some people take years before they climb down. Some take months. Some weeks. Some days. Some hours (that's better). Some minutes. And some seconds. If you can narrow the time gap to seconds, you can often catch yourself before you say what you started to say.

This is how one gets to know God's ways. You can almost sense the fluttering of the wings of the Dove! I know what it is to say to myself, "If I finish this sentence, I will chase the Dove away." So I stop! I don't say it.

I need to repeat here that we are talking about a metaphor when we speak of the Dove flying away. Never forget that the Holy Spirit never leaves us—ever. But we may lose the *sense* of His anointing; we lose the presence of mind that God wants each of us to have all the time.

Here's my third point about God's ways: *walk in the light that God gives you.* A most relevant verse is this: "But if we walk in the light as He is in the light, we have fellowship one with another, and the blood of Jesus Christ His Son cleanses us from all sin" (1 John 1:7). This verse—written for Christians—is not an instruction on how to stay saved. No. Salvation is secure. No worries there. But fellowship with the Father is offered on the condition that we walk in the light God gives us.

What does walking in the light mean? For one thing, it is all I said above with regard to getting rid of bitterness by practicing total forgiveness. This is light that God has shone on your path. If you don't walk in it, but go outside of it, you will be in darkness where there is no fellowship with the Father. Walk in the light. Get rid of bitterness. Forgive.

---

*The Holy Spirit never leaves us—ever. But
we may lose the sense of His anointing;
we lose the presence of mind that God
wants each of us to have all the time.*

But sometimes there is more. God may confront you with a responsibility that you know you must accept if you are going to move forward with the Lord. In my own case,

I came to a crossroad in 1982 when I was the minister of Westminster Chapel. I had invited Arthur Blessitt to minister to us for the entire month of May. I had no idea that he would get us on the streets and make us witness to everybody in our path! That was beyond my wildest dream! I only wanted Arthur to preach and encourage us. But he got us on the streets.

And one evening—I will never forget it—I was confronted with a vision of a pilot light—a light that stays lit in a gas oven. I knew I would have to lead Westminster Chapel into a ministry of personal evangelism. I always thought I was doing my job by preaching from the pulpit! By the way, it is a lot easier to speak to hundreds than to one person. On that evening in May 1982, I died a thousand deaths: "My ambitions, plans and wishes, at my feet in ashes lay."[2] I was never to be the same again. I walked in the light God gave me. We launched the Pilot Light ministry in June 1982—witnessing every Saturday to passersby on the streets of Victoria between Big Ben and Buckingham Palace. It was a milestone in my Westminster ministry.

I could have refused to walk in that light. Had I done so, I would have succumbed to pigeon religion. I dare say, had I refused to begin to talk to people personally about Jesus— and not just from the pulpit—God would have put me to one side and I would never have been heard of again. I shudder to think what life would have been like had I not walked in the light.

What God required of me may be different from what He requires of you. But *you will know* when God is shedding light on your path. He may ask you to do what has not been done before. There may be no precedent. But you will know if it is from Him. Meanwhile, take hold with both hands when God shows what you ought to be doing. Gladly accept any insight into yourself you had not seen before. God may show you a malady in yourself that has always been there but to which you for some reason have been blind. Confess any sin you become conscious of. Obey any impulse that you honestly believe could only have been put there by the Holy Spirit.

This is a vital part of getting to know God's ways.

Fourth, *replace grumbling with gratitude.* The generation of Israelites that God swore in His wrath would not enter into His rest (Heb. 3:11) is the same generation Paul calls grumblers. "Do not grumble, as some of them did—and were killed by the destroying angel" (1 Cor. 10:10, NIV).

Midway in my ministry at Westminster Chapel, I came to see the importance of gratitude. It was a case of walking in the light that was equal to starting our Pilot Light ministry. As a result of preaching on Philippians 4:6—"In every situation, by prayer and petition, with thanksgiving, present your requests to God" (NIV)—I was suddenly convicted of my own unthankfulness. I repented as I had never done, realizing how I should be the most thankful person on Earth but barely said "Thank You" to God—even for the most obvious things. I vowed to change. I did. I never looked back. From that day to this, I have kept my vow to be a thankful man.

I discovered three things:

1. God loves gratitude. He wants us to say "Thank You" for the smallest and biggest things He does for us.

2. God hates ingratitude. He notices it when we do not say "Thank You." When ten lepers were healed and only one came back to say "Thank You," Jesus immediately asked, "Were not all ten cleansed? Where are the other nine?" (Luke 17:17, NIV).

3. Gratitude must be taught. I immediately began to preach on thankfulness to my church in Westminster. Not only that; at our prayer meetings we took time out to ask for nothing but only list things for which we were grateful.

> It changed the spirit of our prayer meetings
> and changed many lives.

Suggestion: think of three things for which you are thankful to God before you go to bed each night. Or do it each morning as you reflect upon the previous day. Chances are, more than three things will come to your mind! "Count your blessings, name them one by one, and it will surprise you what the Lord has done."[3]

God loves gratitude. But there is another reason to be grateful: more and more research shows that being thankful has positive effects on your health and well-being.[4]

God wants us to develop into being a thankful people; it is one of His ways. The ancient Israelites were not that. If you knew how much God hates grumbling—murmuring and complaining—I think you would stop it immediately!

Fifth, *never run ahead of God*. One does not want to lag behind, neither do we want to proceed without Him. The ancient Israelites were trained not to move unless the cloud lifted.

> And on the day that the tabernacle was erected, the cloud covered the tabernacle, the tent of the testimony, and at evening there was over the tabernacle the appearance of fire until the morning. So it was always. The cloud covered it by day, and the appearance of fire by night. When the cloud was lifted up from over the tabernacle, then after it the children of Israel journeyed, and in the place where the cloud settled, there the children of Israel camped. At the commandment of the LORD the children of Israel journeyed, and at the commandment of the LORD they camped. As long as the cloud dwelt over the tabernacle they camped. When the cloud remained many days over the tabernacle, then the children of Israel kept the charge of the LORD and did not

journey. When the cloud remained a few days over the tabernacle, according to the commandment of the LORD they dwelt in their tents, and according to the commandment of the LORD they journeyed. When the cloud dwelt from evening until morning and the cloud was lifted up in the morning, then they journeyed. Whether it was by day or by night that the cloud was lifted up, they journeyed. Whether it was two days, or a month, or a long time that the cloud dwelt over the tabernacle, the children of Israel dwelt in their tents and did not journey. But when it was lifted up they journeyed. At the command of the LORD they camped, and at the command of the LORD they journeyed. They kept the charge of the LORD at the command of the LORD by the hand of Moses.

—NUMBERS 9:15–23

It must have gotten very boring at times, having to remain in one place in the wilderness for a long time. Yet there comes a time when God says, "Stay."

Joseph and Mary made the mistake of thinking Jesus was with them when He wasn't; they moved ahead of Him.

When the days of the feast were complete, as they returned, the Child Jesus remained behind in Jerusalem. And Joseph and His mother did not know of it. But supposing Him to be in their company, they went a day's journey. Then they searched for Him among their relatives and acquaintances. When they did not find Him, they returned to Jerusalem, searching for Him. After three days they found Him in the temple, sitting in the midst of the teachers, listening to them and asking them questions.

—LUKE 2:43–46

L–O–V–E

I want to share an acrostic that I have come up with for my personal use. I literally pray every single day that I will not grieve the Holy Spirit. I try to apply this acrostic all day long— whether with the general public or at home. This works for me, although I so often fall short:

L — let be

O — overlook

V — become vulnerable

E — emancipate

Let be. This means to accept things as they are. In Richard Baxter's hymn "Ye Holy Angels Bright," there is a line, "Take what He gives."[5] This means to accept without complaining what God allows to take place, including disappointment or bad news. Let it be. Leave it alone. Don't try to change things or knock down a door that is suddenly closed to you. Let God work for you.

Overlook. This refers to the behavior of rude, thoughtless people. They may insult you or accuse you. A driver may cut in front of you without warning and you feel like getting even by doing the same thing to him or her. Overlook it. Don't try to get even. It is what Jesus meant by turning the other cheek (see Matthew 5:39). The Bible also says not to answer a fool according to his folly or you are as bad as he is (see Proverbs 26:4).

Vulnerable. Become vulnerable. Be willing to look like a wimp. Don't defend yourself. You don't have to look strong. Let the mind of Christ govern you. He who was God "emptied Himself" (Phil. 2:7). In the King James Version, this verse says Jesus "made himself of no reputation." Be willing, therefore, to become a nobody.

Emancipate. This is probably the hardest to apply. This means you say what it takes to set them free. It is when you are in a situation in which the other person is clearly in the wrong. You know it and they know it. Instead of playing "Gotcha," you let them save face. This is graciousness in the extreme. But that is the way God is!

I can safely promise that you will avoid grieving the Spirit if you live by these principles. It will also help you to keep from running ahead of God.

One of the easiest things in the world to do is to run ahead of God. If Joseph and Mary could do it, so can we. In my book *Sensitivity of the Spirit,* I spend a lot of time explaining how Joseph and Mary ran ahead of the Lord when they thought He was with them. It is so easy to do. Sadly, pigeon religion can creep in and envelop us when we do not realize this has happened.

Part of getting to know God's ways is being able to detect the first appearance of pigeon religion. It is easier to lose the anointing than it is to get it back. That is one of the things Joseph and Mary learned. If we cause the lifting of the Dove but still carry on, it means that we have sadly embraced pigeon religion.

Once you realize you have run ahead of the Lord and have left Him behind, immediately start looking for Him. Don't keep going ahead. That would be embracing pigeon religion.

Don't let pigeon religion motivate you!

Chapter 4

THE ANOINTING

But the anointing which you have received from Him remains in
you, and you do not need anyone to teach you. For as the same
anointing teaches you concerning all things, and is truth, and
is no lie, and just as it has taught you, remain in Him.

—1 JOHN 2:27

———◆———

Pigeons will eat "junk" food.
Doves eat only seeds and fruit.

———◆———

ONE OF THE most hilarious moments of my life was when Lyndon Bowring, Rob Parsons, and I were asked to sit on the front row of a London church to hear a preacher who was well known for his prophetic gift. We had slipped in to sit on the back row because we could not stay for the entire service. But the man chairing the meeting spotted us and made us come down to the front—all before a thousand people. But that is not what I remember most. When the speaker began to preach, I noticed him looking at me a lot, and I had been struggling to smile and affirm him. I knew it was affecting him. I felt sorry for him. I wrote Lyndon a note: "This man is in bondage to me. Please say something to make me smile." A minute later Lyndon handed me a note. I cannot remember exactly what he said. I look forward to reading it in heaven. All I can say is, I burst out laughing.

My shoulders shook uncontrollably. I feared the congregation would see me looking irreverent. But his note worked.
I was able to smile with great freedom. Within a minute the
preacher began to prophesy to me. He guaranteed the most
amazing anointing coming to me, including my reaching all
sorts of important people, including heads of state. My two
friends got prophesied to as well. The three of us went out to
eat afterward, trying to assess whether the man we heard was
truly anointed, or practicing pigeon religion.

The word *anointing* is a tricky term. This is because it is
used in more than one way. For example, King Saul was
always regarded as "the LORD's anointed" by David (1 Sam.
24:6), even though the Lord "had departed from" Saul (1 Sam.
18:12). Being "the Lord's anointed" in those days meant that
the anointing oil had been poured on the man chosen as
king; he remained king throughout his life.

The Greek word for anointing is *chrisma*—not *charisma*;
the latter is a different word although the two words look
and sound alike. *Chrisma* comes from the root word *chrio*
from which we get "Christ"—the Anointed One. The word
chrio contains the idea of "smearing as with an ointment."
As for *charisma*, it has become a popular word in the media
and politics for many years. You can probably get elected
to political office nowadays if you have "charisma"—a certain something that people, especially the press, seem to
recognize. The sad thing about charisma is that it sometimes fits well with pigeon religion; one can easily have charisma without *chrisma*—the anointing of the Holy Spirit.
So many TV preachers have charisma; it is often taken for
the anointing. As some cannot tell the difference between a
pigeon and a dove, so too many of us do not know the difference between charisma and the anointing.

And yet there is still another word—*charismata*: grace-
gift. This is the word used for the gifts of the Holy Spirit
in 1 Corinthians 12, for example. Believe it or not, you can

also have the charismata without the anointing—that is, the anointing as I am about to define it.

In this chapter I use the word *anointing* in three ways. First, the anointing is enjoying God's manifest *approval*. This is what King Saul lost even though he remained king. This sense of the anointing is when you please God; it is when you are conscious of His presence, pleasure, and communication with you. It is what provides insight, presence of mind, wisdom, and clear thinking. Second, the anointing is that which flows with *ease* in a person. You don't have to work it up; it comes easily. If I go outside of my anointing, I struggle. When I stay within my anointing, my gift functions with ease. Therefore, when the anointing flourishes, one exercises his or her gift without stress or effort. But let that anointing diminish, and one will struggle and have to work hard. Third, the word *anointing* can sometimes be used interchangeably with one's ability or *gift*.

To return to my main point: there is a sense in which you can have charisma (a striking personality) and the charismata (grace-gift) without the *chrisma* anointing. As I said, King Saul lost God's approval. But strange as it may seem, he retained the charismata. He was turned into a different person. The Bible says "God gave him another heart" and he was given the gift of prophecy (1 Sam. 10:9–10). People were in awe. They said, "Is Saul also among the prophets?" (1 Sam. 10:11). Sometime later, after young David had become such a threat, Saul sought to kill David. On his way to kill David, Saul began to prophesy again (1 Sam. 19:23–24)! This proves that the charismata—grace-gift—can remain in a person even though one has lost God's approval.

Therefore, when you hear of people whose ministries continue to flourish even though they have fallen into sin and bring disgrace on God's name, hopefully you will remember the teaching in this book and it will help to explain why and how this can happen. It seems that every day a Christian minister somewhere in the world is exposed in some type of sexual sin. But their gift flourished the whole time they were living in sin. They continue to prophesy, preach, give spectacular words of knowledge, and—would you believe it—even see people healed. It is because, as I mentioned earlier, the gifts and calling of God are irrevocable (Rom. 11:29).

How does this happen? I cannot be sure. But consider this scenario: a minister is greatly used—whether by powerful preaching, prophesying, giving words of knowledge, or healing—but somehow gives into temptation. It could be temptation with regard to sex or misuse of money. Whatever. The minister then succumbs to temptation. But, strangely enough, he or she notices that their gift still functions! The minister says, "Apparently God is not displeased with me or I would not have the same power" and continues to give in to temptation and carry on in ministry. His or her gift continues to flourish. It becomes a lifestyle until he or she gets caught. And unfortunately, many continue right on even *after* they've been caught, whether they truly repent or not.

JUNK FOOD

As I said at the beginning of this chapter, pigeons eat anything, but doves eat only healthy food. If we pursue the authentic anointing, we must stick to a diet that is healthy. For example, how much do you read your Bible? How important is *knowing* the Bible to you? Job said, "I have esteemed the words of His mouth more than my necessary food" (Job 23:12).

People who prefer secular magazines to Scripture, reading gossip to praying, or being acquainted with the latest news rather than spending time alone with God are like pigeons who eat anything—junk food. They "feed" their spirits with whatever garbage they find.

A close relative of junk food is fast food. I don't think it is particularly healthy to always be chasing after a *rhema* word. The worldly equivalent is people who read their horoscope or call a psychic hotline. My prophetic friends have told me of the perpetual annoyance they endure by people coming up to them asking for a "word." To me, this is the spiritual equivalent of fast food. It smacks of people who are always in a hurry, going to McDonald's or Burger King. "Make it quick. I don't have time to pray or read my Bible, so just give me what I want."

What kind of spiritual diet do you have? How much do you read your Bible? How much time do you spend in social media? Do you spend more time reading Facebook than the Good Book? This can be a very unhealthy addiction.

It is easier to read the newspaper than to read the Bible. It is easier to watch television than it is to pray. But not having a solid spiritual diet sets one up to accept lies in place of the truth. It makes one more susceptible to pigeon religion.

Many years ago Dr. Martyn Lloyd-Jones introduced me to *Robert Murray M'Cheyne's Bible Reading Calendar.* I would not take anything in the world in exchange for the good that has come to me from this plan. I have now read the Bible some forty times. A famous preacher told me he has yet to read the Bible all the way through. I know that some preachers only consult the Bible when they need to prepare a sermon. Never forget that the Bible is the Holy Spirit's greatest product! The Holy Spirit wrote Holy Scripture (1 Tim. 3:16; 2 Pet. 1:21). If you want to get on good terms with the Holy Spirit, then get to know His Word! The *logos*, not merely *rhema*! Any Bible reading plan is good. You can go online and find a wide selection of one-year Bible reading plans. Start today! This is the sure way to invite the Dove—not the pigeon—into your life if you really and truly want to know God.

BE SLOW TO POINT THE FINGER

I want to make a few more points about ministry leaders who get involved in sexual promiscuity or financial mismanagement. Some enter into very shady financial dealings. Some pay themselves huge salaries that come from the love offerings of (in some cases) poor people. They live in luxury while promising their congregants prosperity if they continue to give. Pigeon religion.

They think they get away with it! And they do—for a while. Sooner or later such deeds will be exposed. King Saul remained king for some twenty years. This meant his evil efforts went on and on and on—and God apparently did nothing.

But when you consider their final destiny, that they are on slippery ground (see Psalm 73:17–18), you realize that God eventually steps in and judges them. The end can in some cases be pathetic beyond adequate words to describe. Consider Saul's end: suicide (1 Sam. 31:4).

Do you not find this very strange—that God allows unworthy ministers to flourish for so long? I know that I do. But, that said, I have to come clean and admit that God has been extremely patient with me. I write this book as an unworthy man. God has been so gracious to me that it is embarrassing. How can God be so good to such unworthy people? All I know is that His ways are higher than our ways, and I am happy to leave it at that.

When I was a teenager, one of my preacher heroes would come to my church in Ashland, Kentucky, every year or so. At the time I thought he was one of the most powerful preachers I ever heard. He had what seemed to be amazing power and authority when he stepped into the pulpit. Seldom had a sense of the fear of God fallen on a congregation as when he would preach. I am so glad I had no idea then what was going on behind the scenes. I discovered years later that a woman who was not his wife would follow him wherever he went—all over the United States. She would register separately and stay in the same hotel. Their affair went on for a long time, until one day he was found out. His ministry ended immediately. And yet many people had been converted through this man's ministry.

As I mentioned, in some cases a ministry does not end when a person is exposed for sexual or financial impropriety.

It continues with little or no disruption. First, people are more forgiving nowadays than they used to be. Second, some have no sense of shame. They either deny what was happening or say, "God has forgiven me," and carry on without any restitution or need for discipline.

The God of the Bible is a gracious God. He is slow to anger (Exod. 34:6–7). He has been patient with all of us. It is by the sheer grace of God that any of us has been kept from falling. It has taught me to be patient with others. Whenever I hear of a fellow minister falling I say, "That could be me. There go I but by the grace of God."

Therefore God can give His anointing to whomever He is pleased to give it. And if He looked for a reason to withhold that anointing in *any* of us, He would be totally justified in granting no mercy whatever. Let us therefore be patient with one another and be slow to point the finger.

These things said, God is no respecter of persons. Even David, a man after God's own heart, eventually fell into the grossest possible sins—adultery and murder. But he was caught. Found out. And severely chastened.

If, then, God grants any of us any measure of His anointing, we should know it is not according to our good works but according to His own purpose and grace. This should keep us from arrogance and taking ourselves too seriously.

High Level of Anointing

The anointing I dream of has not come to me so far. Two times in my life a high level of anointing came close to what I have always wanted. First, when I was preaching in Bimini, Bahamas. Bimini is one of the great spots in the world for bonefishing. The legendary "Bonefish Sam" was alive then. He took me fishing many times, and we even won the Bimini Native Tournament in 1969.

Sam was also a serious believer in Jesus Christ. He began preaching in a small church in Bailey Town, Bimini. I was invited to preach there on a Sunday evening. During the service, all of the Bahamian congregation of about twenty got on our knees to worship. I wondered what I should speak on.

All of a sudden it came to me: "Jesus Christ is the same yesterday, and today, and forever" (Heb. 13:8). The presence of the Lord was so real, taking me back to the day I was initially baptized with the Spirit in 1955. I was allowed to see in what sense Jesus is the "same." For one thing, He *looks* the same. His face has not changed. His body has not changed. He still has the nail prints in His hands and side.

The anointing I dream of has not come to me so far. Two times in my life a high level of anointing came close to what I have always wanted.

I later stood up to preach. Never before was I given such anointing. After that service I said, "Lord, why didn't You give me this anointing this morning when I was at Coral Ridge Presbyterian Church in Fort Lauderdale ministering to two thousand people? Why don't You give me this anointing in Westminster Chapel?" But no. He did it for those precious souls in Bimini. Dove religion took over. They never forgot that night.

Second, only once in twenty-five years at Westminster Chapel did I have an undoubted taking over of the Holy Spirit on my preaching. To be honest, yes, I know I had a measure of anointing over the twenty-five years. But nothing compared with that morning. God stepped in and took over. I was almost like a spectator. The text was Philippians 1:12: "I want you to know, brothers, that the things which happened to me have resulted in advancing the gospel." I was conscious of an ability, authority, and power like I had never experienced in that pulpit. When the sermon was over and I sat down next to the pulpit after the final hymn, I thought to myself, "Well. That was amazing." Two hours later one of our deacons nervously approached me and said, "Dr. Kendall, I have some disappointing news. Your sermon this morning was not recorded. The man who is in charge of the recordings was ill and forgot to let us know he could not be at church." That was that. Why? You tell me.

FINDING OUR ANOINTING

I said earlier that there is a third use of the word *anointing*: when it pertains to one's ability or gift. That is our focus now.

The hardest thing about discovering our anointing is coming to terms with our limits. This has been the most difficult and humbling journey for me. I sometimes think I have been given a double dose of pride that is far out of proportion to my anointing. A long time ago I realized that though I loved their theology, I am no John Calvin and I am no Jonathan Edwards. Furthermore, following in the footsteps of the greatest preacher of the twentieth century, that I am no Martyn Lloyd-Jones. As to why God put me in Westminster Chapel, I cannot be sure, although I know He did. My point is, I have had to come to terms with my limits.

After all, each of us is only given a "measure" of faith. Only Jesus had the Holy Spirit without measure—without any limit (John 3:34). Since we are only given a measure of faith, we are told not to think of ourselves more highly than we should (Rom. 12:3). This surely means we should also think of ourselves as much as we should. In any case, it can be a very humbling process.

There are two parts of our gifting or anointing: (1) that which comes by creation and the way we were brought up, and (2) that which comes as a result of conversion—faith in Christ. It is the latter we deal with in this chapter. And yet in order to discover our anointing, we must begin with the way we are made—what is given us by creation. In other words, that which seems natural. All of us have some kind of natural ability or talent. That is a good place to begin when you want to discover your anointing.

Do not ask yourself, "What would I like to be?" Ask, "What am I good at?" Your natural talent is often a hint as to how God wants you to spend your life. God created you, choosing not only your parents but also the place of your birth (Acts 17:26). This means He is behind what you are good at. We are all shaped by heredity and environment. Furthermore, God has always been looking over our shoulders throughout our childhood, eavesdropping on every conversation and—do try to accept this—ordering our lives in every detail. This includes what He allows that we feel was so negative. It is all part of bringing us to the place we are today. We need, therefore, to accept the way God made us.

So do ask yourself what you do well. Your natural abilities—those things that come easy for you—are fairly strong hints about how God will use you. For the anointing is something that does not need to be "worked up"; it comes with ease.

All of us have some kind of natural ability or talent. That is a good place to begin when you want to discover your anointing.

Your natural ability combined with the fact you have been born again leads to your true anointing—your gift or talent being used for the Lord. What you are called to do is what you will be enabled to do.

God never promotes us to the level of our incompetence. Perhaps you have read the book *The Peter Principle*. The thesis of the book is, every person is promoted to the level of his or her incompetence. Many people want the better job for the prestige and the money. But when they get it, they struggle or fail. The secretary was good at typing letters but was out of her depth when made manager of the office. The vice president was doing fine until he was made president; he soon had burnout and could not cope.

But God does not do this. He will never promote you to

the level of your incompetence. Charles Spurgeon said that if God calls you to preach, He will give you a pair of lungs. By that he meant that if God opens a door it is because you will be equipped for the new task.

King Saul: An Example of Yesterday's Man

A part of King Saul's folly stemmed from the fact that he wasn't content merely to be king. He wanted to function as a priest as well. His initial downfall came when he became impatient while waiting for Samuel to show up as promised. Samuel was delayed. It would be Samuel's duty alone to offer the burnt offering—not Saul's. But Saul apparently said to himself, "I am king, aren't I? I can do what I please." So he ordered, "Bring here to me the burnt offering and the peace offerings" (1 Sam. 13:9). Huge mistake. King Saul consciously went right against the ceremonial law which states that only the priest called of God could administer the burnt and fellowship offerings. Anyone else doing these things should be "put to death" (Num. 3:10). So King Saul offered the burnt offerings. When he finished, Samuel turned up and said, "What have you done?" (1 Sam. 13:11).

Saul knew exactly what he had done—going right against the Word of God. The king became defensive, almost blaming his decision on the Lord! "I forced myself, and offered the burnt offering." Imagine that. Another translation says he "felt compelled." This is not unlike people who say, "God told me to do this," even though it is right against Holy Scripture. I've known people to say, "I don't care what the Bible says; I know when I hear from God." In any case, King Saul justified himself for his action.

> Samuel said to Saul, "You have done foolishly. You have not kept the commandment of the Lord your God, which He commanded you. Truly now, the

LORD would have established your kingdom over
Israel forever. But now your kingdom will not continue. The LORD has sought for Himself a man after
His own heart and the LORD has commanded him
to be prince over His people, because you have not
kept that which the LORD commanded you."

—1 SAMUEL 13:13–14

You should know that this was not a one-off incident in
Holy Writ. Later on, King Uzziah fell into the same folly. He
became powerful and "his pride led to his downfall." He
entered the temple of the Lord to burn incense on the altar
of incense. Azariah the priest confronted him and said, "It
is not for you, Uzziah, to burn incense to the LORD for it is
for the priests…you have been unfaithful" (2 Chron. 26:18).
Immediately leprosy broke out on the king's forehead. "King
Uzziah had leprosy until the day of his death" (2 Chron. 26:21).
Uzziah had been a great king in many ways. But he was remembered for this: "He is a leper" (2 Chron. 26:16–23). All knew it
was the judgment of God. God is no respecter of persons.

King Saul became yesterday's man when he was only forty.
He remained king for another twenty years. Think of this:
he wore the crown without the anointing for the rest of his
reign. The people did not know what Samuel knew: that Saul
had been rejected by God as king even though he remained
king (1 Sam. 16:1).

This also shows that God can judge in more than one
way. With King Saul there was no instant death; with Uzziah
there was immediate evidence of judgment that led to death.

THE GIFTS OF THE SPIRIT

One of the more puzzling and yet explainable phenomena
regarding King Saul is how he was given the gift of prophecy
and kept it after the anointing was lifted from him. First, he
was changed into another man: "God gave him another heart"

(1 Sam. 10:9). Second, he was given the gift of prophecy: "the Spirit of God came upon him, and he prophesied among them." So stunning was his gift that those around him said, "Is Saul also among the prophets?" (1 Sam. 10:10, 12). Third, the anointing lifted from Saul; he became what I call "yesterday's man" in a very short period of time (1 Sam. 16:1; 18:12). Fourth, Saul became obsessed with young David and lived day and night to kill him (1 Sam. 19:9–19). Fifth, on his way to kill David, lo and behold, the Spirit of God came upon him again and the refrain was repeated: "Is Saul also among the prophets?" (1 Sam. 19:20, 24).

Is this not amazing? King Saul, now without the approval of God and trying to kill David, still has this gift of prophecy? It is a mystery, except for this explanation that the Apostle Paul brings out: "the gifts and calling of God are irrevocable" (Rom. 11:29). In other words, He gives these gifts without conditions. Godliness does not guarantee that God will grant a gift of the Spirit; ungodliness will not forfeit the gift once you have it. Strange as it may seem, that is the way it is.

If you believe in the gifts of the Spirit and their availability for our day, this should give you pause. It is a grim reminder that the gifts are no certain proof of one's spirituality. You could therefore speak in tongues, have the gift of prophecy, miracles, and healing—and live an ungodly life. Further proof of this is how high-profile religious leaders can live double lives and still see miracles in their ministries. I once talked with a man who was found out but then repented of his homosexual lifestyle. I asked him, "Did your gift flourish in all your carryings on?" He replied: "Yes."

King Saul became yesterday's man but wore the crown for another twenty years. We must keep his example in mind when we observe strange things in our time. It is a mystery. I don't understand it. But one can be yesterday's man (or woman) and appear to be today's man (or woman) and live a double life.

And yet the greater problem is this: so many people do

not have discernment to recognize pigeon religion. Jesus said that in the last days "false christs and false prophets will arise and show great signs and wonders to deceive, if possible, even the elect" (Matt. 24:24).

The surest way to become yesterday's man or woman is to take Scripture lightly. You may say that the Bible is out of date—to your peril. Don't go there. The Word of God is eternal in the heavens; God has not taken back what He wrote and is not ashamed of any part of it. Don't be ashamed of Holy Scripture.

The moment we play fast and loose with the Word of God will be the moment we open the door for pigeon religion. And you can be sure the pigeon will waste no time flying in.

Chapter 5

EVANGELICAL PIGEONS

Having a form of godliness, but denying its power.
—2 TIMOTHY 3:5

Pigeons are territorial. Doves are not territorial.

P IGEON RELIGION MAY show up in surprising places. Do you think that abuses of the Holy Spirit are carried out only by Charismatics or Pentecostals? Hardly. Pigeon religion may show up in any number of places. Whether in the cathedrals of Europe or the megachurches in the United States, whether in Rome or in Dallas, whether in tongues-speaking house churches in Britain or in cessationist Reformed churches in America. Pigeon religion is no respecter of theology.

We originally moved to England so I could study at Oxford. My research took me many times to the British Library in London. I will never forget a particular moment there as long as I live. I had been reading the sermons of Thomas Hooker (1586–1647) for days. Thomas Hooker was the founder of the state of Connecticut. But his theology is permeated with what I now call pigeon religion. His central theme was "preparation for faith," namely, one had to be "prepared" before he could claim to have true faith. This preparation consisted of becoming sanctified even before one was saved! One needed a complete change of life before he could claim the promise of salvation.

Whereas the sixteenth century Reformers (such as Luther and Calvin) taught that one was justified by faith *alone*, many of the English Puritans of the seventeenth century brought in a new dimension: how do you know you have true faith? Instead of faith assuring a person by looking directly to Jesus Christ as the Reformers taught, you need to be sure you have genuine faith by looking within before you could claim to be saved. The result was that one looked to his works for his salvation to be firm. This led to people never knowing whether they were saved because they always feared they did not have enough good works to prove they had genuine faith.

One afternoon as I read all I could take of Hooker's kind of thinking, I asked myself, "Is this why I have come to England? Is this what I am supposed to preach? Is this why I left my old denomination? This is the kind of legalism I was set free from. I might as well have *stayed* there." I pushed my chair back and stared at the ceiling. I could not wait to get out of the British Library that day. What I now call pigeon religion was precisely what some of these Puritans were espousing. It was a turning point for me.

It also gave me a fairly sharp theological perception in discerning what (to me) was solid teaching and what isn't. It became the foundation of all I taught during my twenty-five years in London—and all I have taught since. It also led me in a direction that some sincere godly people found uncomfortable. But I understood them.

Any kind of theology can lead a person or community of believers into being territorial, into feeling a certain area is "ours." It belongs to *us*. We don't want anyone intruding. We will defend our territory, even attack if someone comes into an area we believe is ours. Barracudas are territorial; bonefish are not. Pigeons are territorial; doves are not.

I came across territorial "pigeons" all the time. But I became territorial too!

Robert Amess, a close friend, was pastor of Duke Street Baptist Church in Richmond, London, while I was at Westminster Chapel. He is Reformed the same as I am but has always been more accepted by the Reformed community. I wondered why until Robert told me, "They think you stole Westminster Chapel from them." I found this helpful. Robert was right. The truth is, I had begun to feel the same way; I felt the Chapel belonged to me.

A minister may feel that the pulpit in which he preaches is peculiarly *his*. A church member may feel that where he or she sits in church is "my seat." Woe to a visitor who gets there first! A pastor who has been in the same church for years may feel that nobody else could ever belong there. If he also wants to be the greatest pastor ever, it becomes difficult for someone to follow him. He wants to ensure that he is remembered more than all those before him.

One of the greatest preachers who ever lived somehow allowed pigeon religion to nest in his ego. A patriarch and a revered mentor of many, this man had been in his church for many years, although a number of his friends thought it was time for him to go. They offered him everything from a trip around the world to a bronze statue of himself if he would retire. He accepted the bronze statue—but would not resign! With his full oversight and instructions, they hired one of the greatest sculptors in the world. The famed pastor only had one more request, that his bronze statue not be placed in the open air. "I have seen what the pigeons do to Lord Nelson in London's Trafalgar Square. I do not want pigeons defecating on my head."

I was surprised when I heard this. I had admired him so much. I can't imagine allowing a statue of oneself to be made. I would have thought he would turn down an offer like that and instead let people honor him after he is in heaven.

It reminds me of the only two people in the Old Testament who made monuments to themselves while still living—King

Saul (1 Sam. 15:12) and Absalom, David's son (2 Sam. 18:18). Both of these men's lives came to tragic ends.

CESSATIONISM

The esteemed preacher to whom I have just referred is a cessationist to his fingertips. He is absolutely a good man. I still admire him. Cessationists by and large are good, godly men. They are in a sense the salt of the earth. They are often the sole vanguards of Christian orthodoxy. I don't know what we would do without them. We need them more than ever—if only they would make room for the Holy Spirit! Cessationists, sadly, do not believe in the availability of the gifts of the Spirit in the church today. As much as I admire them, I would not be honest if I did not bring them into this book. Let no one think, therefore, that only Charismatics succumb to pigeon religion.

Is cessationism truly a manifestation of pigeon religion? Yes. I'm sorry, but as I said, cessationism is the view that the gifts of the Holy Spirit—signs, wonders, and miracles— *ceased* at some time before the closing of the canon of Scripture in the early fourth century. It is only a hypothesis. There is not a hint of this teaching in Scripture. But when cessationists turn their hypothesis into a dogma, it is a dead giveaway that pigeon religion moved in.

Cessationists hold a view of the Spirit that is merely *soteriological*, meaning they believe the Spirit is effectual in salvation. They believe in the Trinity, yes. They are thoroughly orthodox when it comes to the essentials of the Christian faith. But they have no place for an immediate and direct witness of the Spirit of God. They quench the Spirit before He has opportunity to act! They believe the Holy Spirit only *applies* the Word. The notion of the Holy Spirit speaking directly to us as He did to Philip in Acts 8:29 is out of the question. They certainly and rightly believe that one cannot be converted apart from the Holy Spirit (John 6:44), but they have no place for the Holy Spirit's *own* witness. Dr. Martyn Lloyd-Jones used to stress to me the importance of the words "immediate and direct" when it comes to the Holy Spirit. Not "mediate" or "indirect"—which is a soteriological understanding of the Spirit. But the "immediate and direct witness of the Holy Spirit," he used to stress to me. Those who want more details should have a look at my book *Holy Fire* in which are two chapters on cessationism.

Cessationism is partly a fulfillment of some of the conditions Paul said would be evident in the last days: "having a form of godliness, but denying its power" (2 Tim 3:5). To a cessationist, Jesus manifested His power two thousand years ago but not today. The Holy Spirit demonstrated power two thousand years ago but not today. And yet Jesus Christ is the same "yesterday, and today, and forever" (Heb. 13:8). And so too the Holy Spirit.

Cessationism is a view that encourages mainly intellectual belief. It is mostly cerebral. It tends to be suspicious of anything emotional. Some cessationists actually dismiss most Charismatics and Pentecostals as being unsaved and never converted. This is pigeon religion and is, in my candid opinion, dangerous teaching. I would not want to be in the shoes of anybody who says that speaking in tongues is "voodoo."

Here is an amazing quote from C. S. Lewis: "We seldom find the Christian miracles denied except by those who have abandoned some part of the Christian doctrines. The mind which asks for a non-miraculous Christianity is a mind relapsing from Christianity into mere 'religion.'"[1] Whereas he was almost certainly speaking of liberal theologians, it is nonetheless true that cessationists forfeit a vital part of New Testament teaching when they deem the miraculous as virtually impossible today.

A territorial mind-set can cause some of us to take ourselves so seriously that we even form an association or fellowship that includes a certain number of like-minded people; all outside are looked on with suspicion. It is like a new Sanhedrin; we form a group that stands for a certain set of doctrines. All that are sound are in it—that is, if you dot the i's and cross the t's like so. Otherwise we hold you in suspicion! Some of us therefore become theologically territorial; we appear to feel we alone have the right to uphold certain positions.

Pigeon religion, then, can have extremes. You have its abuses within some charismatic evangelical circles; you have it with some noncharismatic evangelicals.

Both can be territorial. We all want to protect our domain! Like pigeons who will attack if another pigeon gets in their way, no one gets a free pass when it comes to being territorial. We all want to protect what we think is "our" territory. We have our mailing lists; don't expect us to share them with anyone! We have our pet theological stance; we don't want someone elbowing in on our doctrinal territory. We find it difficult when someone praises another minister to us. We don't want one of our members attending another church. We need to keep our following intact lest they financially support some other ministry or church.

A territorial mind-set can cause some of us to take ourselves so seriously that we even form an association or fellowship that includes a certain number of like-minded people; all outside are looked on with suspicion.

I'm sorry, but this is what causes rivalry between churches. Between ministries. Between Christian organizations who stand for basically the same truths!

The French atheist Voltaire said, "When it is a question of money, everybody is of the same religion."[2] Alas, many charismatic evangelicals and noncharismatic evangelicals are much the same when it comes to money, getting support, and becoming territorial.

During my time at Westminster Chapel, we made a few changes. As a result of Arthur Blessitt's influence on us, we began doing three things: (1) witnessing on the streets of London between Victoria and Buckingham Palace; (2) singing contemporary Christian choruses and songs as well as the traditional hymns of the church; and (3) inviting people to respond publicly to the preached word. These things had not been done before, and some of the members— all good and godly people—became uneasy.

Opposition to Change

Pigeon religion tried to find its way into Westminster Chapel when we began to make these changes. Opposition was fierce. Some of the older members of the Chapel somehow felt that it was "theirs." They had been attending for years and loved the way it always was. Any deviation from the norm was a threat to them. The funny thing was, it was the singing of choruses that was most offensive to some. There were those who began to oppose my ministry not because of my theology or preaching, or even giving an altar call; it was singing choruses.

When we began some new things at the Chapel, I asked our organist to play spiritual songs and hymns rather than classical music before the services began. Some previous organists played the equivalent of Chopin, Brahms, Beethoven, and Saint-Saëns. Some older members actually felt we were wasting our cherished Willis pipe organ (rumored to be one of the top three organs in London) on choruses. Some actually resented the organist preceding the service with "Turn Your Eyes Upon Jesus" or "He Is Lord" and demanded Chopin—godless though that man was! Strange. Pigeon religion, I think. They said that the classical music was more "worshipful" than modern choruses, even though most of the latter were either taken from the psalms or quoting Scripture!

But the opposite extreme of pigeon religion invaded the Chapel too in those days. Because Arthur Blessitt was perceived as a Charismatic, many Charismatics from all over London came to the Chapel in droves whenever he would be speaking. They took over the front rows and lifted their hands in the air during the singing in an obtrusive and exhibitionist manner—putting off our own people who had been around for years. All the progress I was trying to make in spoon-feeding our people to be more evangelistic, more contemporary, and more open to the Holy Spirit was partially aborted by these people. These "pigeons" were not the slightest bit interested in our expository ministry. They were not interested in our church growing. They did not care about our people having to adjust to what was different for them. They wanted to show us "how it is done" and elbowed their way into the services. They showed only disdain for our members who had been faithful over the years who were sincerely trying to grasp what was going on. I was trying to lead our own people by the hand, but some of these outsiders were scaring our own people away. We lost a lot of good people needlessly. The Dove would have brought peace. Pigeons want to declare war.

But as the saying goes, it takes two to tango. Some of our members did not give our changes a chance. They too declared war, going up to visitors and saying, "You surely don't want to come to this church," scaring the new people away. "There's trouble here," they would say to newcomers. These people also recruited every church member they possibly could in order to oust me. They failed in the end, but those were some of the hardest days we ever experienced.

Our Pilot Lights who gave tracts and ministered to passersby sought to be a blessing. I urged them to smile, be gentle, and give people an opportunity to hear the gospel if possible. We saw a few converts. Not many, but a few. Hundreds prayed the sinner's prayer. Only dozens showed up on Sundays. And those who were converted and started coming to the Chapel were not exactly the aristocracy of London. So our own middle class people—some of them—resented the "type of people" who started coming to the Chapel. Some of our own people were territorial, speaking only to those with whom they were comfortable. This was pigeon religion, people resenting the jobless, the homeless, and those who did not wear the most fashionable clothes. I knew that Jesus would welcome these kinds of people and that if we rejected them we would forfeit the blessing of the Holy Spirit on Westminster Chapel.

Some of my most ardent middle class supporters also turned against my ministry by my preaching from James. All I did was exegete straightforward verses: "Come now, you rich men, weep and howl for your miseries that shall come upon you...the wages that you kept back by fraud from the laborers who harvested your fields are crying..." (James 5:1–4). I was flabbergasted that such a teaching would threaten some people. They *loved* my teaching on justification by faith, freedom from the Law, the blood of Christ propitiating our sins before a just God, and the Law being fulfilled by the death of Christ. They lapped it up. But when I said something that touched their wallets, they left us immediately.

Pigeon religion can therefore show up in any theological position—there are Reformed pigeons as well as Charismatic pigeons—or any denominational culture (Presbyterian, Pentecostal, or Baptist). Whether it be the love of money, sexual lust, or the grab for fame and power, do not be surprised, says Paul: "Satan disguises himself as an angel of light" (2 Cor. 11:14).

Chapter 6

GREED

You lust and do not have, so you kill. You desire to have and cannot obtain. You fight and war. Yet you do not have, because you do not ask.

—JAMES 4:2

———— ❖ ————

Pigeons are greedy. Doves are not greedy.

————‖————

WHEN LOUISE AND I were staying as guests on the premises of the Garden Tomb in Jerusalem, a curious thing happened. It was almost closing time for the day—about ten minutes before five o'clock—when a preacher rang the bell at the door of the Garden Tomb in Jerusalem. He had some boxes with him. The person in the office explained that the Garden Tomb closes at 5:00 p.m. The man insisted that he be let in. Sorry, came the response, it was too late. The preacher would not give up, and they sent for the senior person in charge of the Garden Tomb. The manager also explained that they had to close.

"You must let me in," said the preacher. "I have promised my followers that I would personally carry their requests—which I have right here in these boxes—to the empty tomb and go inside it and pray for their requests," the preacher continued.

"I'm sorry, but we are closed. Do come back tomorrow."

That was it. For some reason the preacher did not return the next day to keep his promise to pray for his followers.

Whatever would motivate a preacher to make a promise like this? Do his followers truly believe that prayers at the Garden Tomb are more likely to be heard in heaven than prayers uttered elsewhere? Does he honestly believe that *his* praying is more effectual than the prayers of his followers? Would he not be doing his followers a far greater favor by teaching *them* to pray for their needs rather than asking them to send in their requests so he could pray for them? And whatever would cause his followers to think that God would take special notice of a request that came from the Garden Tomb?

The Common Denominator Among Charismatics and Pentecostals

The common denominator of Pentecostals and Charismatics fifty years ago was the gifts of the Holy Spirit—signs, wonders, and miracles. Today, for many it is prosperity teaching. This teaching has largely replaced the emphasis on healing and the gifts of the Spirit. Even when healing is highlighted, the focus is often on money.

We all can see what they are doing. They need money to survive. TV time is expensive. If Christians don't support the programs, the ministries will go off the air. Moreover, there are only so many Christians out there. The TV ministers must fish in the Christian pond, and there are only so many fish in that pond. In order to catch the fish, one must come up with offers that will entice the viewer to send in their money. New ideas are needed regarding how to raise money and how to get more people to send in their money. One of those ideas was to offer to pray for people's requests from the Garden Tomb in Jerusalem.

I am not sure which is sadder, offering to pray for people's requests from the Garden Tomb or the fact that people would actually *believe* that God would honor such a request. That people would actually believe a stunt like this suggests an extremely shallow understanding of Holy Scripture. Using this kind of motivation is playing into people's theological ignorance and—I'm sorry—superstition.

And greed. Yes, I'm afraid that greed is sometimes at the bottom of it all. The greedy preacher plays into his greedy viewers. If Jesus showed up today in the manner He did when He came to the temple in ancient Jerusalem, He would head straight for some of these people who don't preach the gospel but think of ways to get people to send in their money. "In the temple He found those who were selling oxen and sheep and doves, and the moneychangers sitting there. When He had made a whip of cords, He drove them all out of the temple, with the sheep and oxen. He poured out the changers' money and overturned the tables. He said to those who sold doves, 'Take these things away! Do not make My Father's house a house of merchandise!'" (John 2:14–16).

Thank God for the exceptions. So the next time you watch any Christian ministry on television, listen carefully. Keep your ears open for any mention of the blood of Jesus Christ turning God's wrath away for our sins. Listen carefully for a message that stresses the need to be born again or that emphasizes having a closer walk with God. Be thankful for the ministry that preaches we are saved by faith alone apart from good works. Listen to see if hell is mentioned, or that we only get to heaven by faith in Jesus Christ. Listen to discover whether the preacher explains verses in the Bible and applies the meaning just for the truth's sake.

I thank God for Christian television. I am thankful for godly preachers and teachers who *do* uphold the gospel on Christian TV—speaking the truth for its own sake—and do not play into people's itching ears. They don't promise the earth and sky for those who support them. They truly are men and women of God who want to see the lost saved and Christians growing in grace.

People who say, "Send in your prayer requests and I will pray for you," surely take themselves too seriously. How dare *anyone* claim to have a fast-track hotline to the throne of God! Not to mention those who give a hint that if you send in an offering you have a better chance of being remembered. The truth is, *anyone* can pray for people.

GOD USES ORDINARY PEOPLE

I recall the story of Jennifer Rees Larcombe. Bound to a wheelchair after a strange virus left her paralyzed for seven years, Jennifer had a teaching ministry all over England, always speaking from her wheelchair. Many people prayed for her to be healed. But one day a young lady who had been saved for only three weeks asked to pray for Jennifer. She was instantly healed and carried her wheelchair home!

You don't need a high-profile faith healer to pray for you.

In the 1950s there was a genuine anointing of healing in certain men and women. There is no doubt about it. Polio, cancer, paralyzed people, the deaf and the mute—no case seemed too difficult. But after a while the anointing lifted. Why? Who knows?

People do get healed nowadays. I have witnessed surprising healings in my own ministry—while at Westminster Chapel and since. Elsewhere I have described my wife's amazing healing. What is more, there are small prayer groups all over the world that pray for people's healing and see them healed! Randy Clark has a wonderful healing ministry, especially in Brazil. Heidi Baker told me of her own miraculous healing at the Airport Christian Fellowship in Toronto. She was so weak that she was literally *carried* by her husband, Rolland, to the pulpit. She then stood up to speak and was instantly healed before the whole congregation! It is a stunning story. Furthermore, she and Rolland see people healed and delivered from the demonic all the time in Mozambique.

I suspect far more people are being healed today under the

ministry of low-profile leaders than under those who have high-profile recognition. Hence the reason I also suspect that so many well-known Charismatics and Pentecostals minimize the ministry of healing and have switched to prosperity teaching. In order to keep money flowing into their ministries, what some TV preachers stoop to is offering "anointed" cloths, or anointing oil that has a secret recipe with the aroma from certain Middle Eastern spices, or merely water from the Jordan River. This practice is disgraceful and is a poor testimony for the Christian faith.

I do believe in my heart of hearts that the day is not far away when God will step in, wake up the church, and restore power to the church as you can read about in the Book of Acts. It is coming. My next book will explain in some detail what I believe will happen when the Word and the Spirit come together—at last. When that happens there will be such an emphasis on the gospel and such power for miracles that it will be hard to say which is focused on more.

DIFFERENT FORMS OF GREED

There is more than one kind of greed. Some are greedy for money. Some are greedy for power and prestige. They can never have enough or be complimented enough. At my first social gathering with Oxford's Faculty of Divinity, I met some of the most brilliant people on the planet—students, dons, professors. I came away thinking one thing to myself: how insecure some of these people seem to be. Some of them have an insatiable need to be admired and applauded for their brilliance.

Pigeons take themselves very seriously. That said, we are all pigeons. I do, however, take a bit of comfort when I recall that Elijah, one of the most powerful prophets in the Old Testament, also took himself too seriously. "I alone remain a prophet of the LORD" (1 Kings 18:22). He was wrong. His example shows that the most anointed of God's people may at times take themselves too seriously. None of us is perfect.

But to make claims that some of us get our prayers through quicker than others—and to offer them virtually for sale—is reprehensible. People who make these claims should get out of the ministry—or repent at once.

Jesus told us to seek first the kingdom of God and His righteousness, and all our needs will be added. What we need—food, shelter, clothing—is part of the package *when* we make the kingdom of God our priority (Matt. 6:33). And what is the kingdom of God? It is the realm and rule of the ungrieved Spirit. If you were to seek *this*, says Jesus, you would get all the other things thrown in! As C. S. Lewis put it, "Aim at Heaven and you will get earth 'thrown in'; aim at earth and you will get neither."[1]

What is so sad is that pigeon religion wants you to make financial needs your priority. Dove religion will lead you to get to know the true and living God for His own sake. Pigeon religion will lead you to focus on what is material. Dove religion will lead you to seek that which is spiritual—getting to know the Lord Jesus Christ in greater measure; getting to know the Bible more than ever; and coming to experience the reality of God's grace that begins with the Cross of Jesus.

The love of money is the root of all evil (1 Tim. 6:10). Jesus said, "Do not store up for yourselves treasures on earth where moth and rust destroy and where thieves break in and steal. But store up for yourselves treasures in heaven, where neither moth nor rust destroy and where thieves do not break in nor steal, for where your treasure is, there will your heart be also" (Matt. 6:19–21). What this means is, focus on heaven; give to God what is *His* and you will lay up treasure in heaven. Live in such a way now that you will be glad about what you did with your money when you get to heaven.

There was a layman I remember in the Church of the Nazarene who made a million dollars. He believed in tithing and gave exactly $100,000 of it to his church—and had receipts to prove it. Sometime later he went bankrupt and lost everything. Some of his friends and family members chided him for what he gave to the church. "I bet you wish you had not given that money to your church," they said to him. His reply: "You are quite wrong; that is the only amount that I *kept*." Tithing is an example of laying up treasure in heaven.

Tithing is God's plan to support the gospel. The first tither was Abraham. He gave spontaneously (Gen. 14:20). But how did he know to give one-tenth? It was revealed to him by the Holy Spirit. Jacob followed the same practice (Gen. 28:22). The ancient patriarchs, then, set the pattern for the way God's work should be supported. But when Mosaic Law came in four hundred years later, tithing was made mandatory. For the Law said that the tithe belongs to the Lord (Lev. 27:30). And yet even under the Law God promised blessing for the obedience: "Bring all the tithes into the storehouse, that there may be food in My house, and test Me now in this, says the LORD of Hosts, if I will not open for you the windows of heaven and pour out for you a blessing, that there will not be room enough to receive it" (Mal. 3:10). The King James Version translates "test me" as "prove me." The nearest God ever comes to proving His existence is when He challenges His people to tithe!

> *Live in such a way now that you will be glad about what you did with your money when you get to heaven.*

What is the storehouse? Ask any rabbi. It was the synagogue. Translating this to the New Testament, the tithe should go to one's own local church or place of worship. If all Christians would tithe, the church throughout the world would be devoid of financial pressures. There would be money to support every missionary—and every television ministry. In my book *Tithing* I make the point that most people do not tithe because they have not been taught. But to those who have been taught tithing—and do not tithe—there is one reason: greed. As we say in Kentucky, "When a feller says, 'It ain't the money; it's the principle,' it's the money."

It is my view that the tithe should be given to one's church. Anything given above the tithe—many can afford to do this—should go to other good causes. But many television evangelists do not want you to know that the storehouse is the local church; they want you to give *them* your money.

There is no doubt that God promises to bless the generous giver. "He who sows sparingly will also reap sparingly, and he who sows bountifully will also reap bountifully" (2 Cor. 9:6). There is also no doubt that God appeals to our self-interest when motiving us to do His will—including giving. My problem with the prosperity teachers is that some of them go to ridiculous extremes to get your money. Let them urge their viewers to give first to their own church and then, if they like, to other ministries.

Godliness with contentment is great gain. But when greed gets in, godliness goes out. Greed is so often at the bottom of pigeon religion. Greed also plays into our weakness to take ourselves too seriously. How? It is because we begin to think that God owes us something, that God should bend His rules for us. We begin to think we are special—that we are the exception to the rule. That is the devil's line! It is Satan who will always appeal to our fragile egos and proneness to greed to get us off track.

James addressed Christian Jews who had become greedy (James 4:1–3). They were never content with what they had, and some of them took it out on the poorer Christians (James 5:1–4). This is why they did not get what they wanted! God did them a favor by keeping them from seeing their greedy desires fulfilled. If you are not seeing your desires fulfilled, it may be God trying to get your attention—to keep you on your knees and seeking His face. Seek His face, and all you need will be added to you. What is more, "Delight yourself in the LORD, and He will give you the desires of your heart" (Ps. 37:4). It doesn't get any better than that.

Chapter 7

THE HERD INSTINCT

But they insisted with loud voices, asking that He be
crucified. And the voices of these men and of the chief priests
prevailed. So Pilate gave the sentence as they demanded.

—LUKE 23:23–24

———— ✦ ————

Pigeons fly as a group. Doves fly solo or in pairs.

————

ARE YOU A Christian? What makes you think you truly are a Christian?

When I was eight years old, I attended a vacation Bible school in a neighboring church in Ashland, Kentucky. A preacher who was very gifted with children gave a sermon. I don't remember the details of the sermon except that it was a sentimental talk that ended with a story that brought us all to tears. We stood for the altar call. I was on a row seated with five girls who were roughly my age. When the girl at the end of the row left her seat to go forward, the other four immediately followed. For some reason this event made an indelible impression on me. Even at that age I had this uncomfortable feeling that these girls did this out of sheer emotion—and were merely sticking together. I have also wondered why I did not follow them.

Years later a famous evangelist was making headlines owing to the number of people who came forward in his meetings. A friend of mine asked him, "I notice that many Christians are the first to walk forward in your meetings when you give the invitation. Why would they do this? They surely don't need to make a decision for Christ."

The evangelist replied, "We have learned that if one or two come forward, others will follow." He had actually requested that a few Christians lead the way when he gave his appeal. Getting the results for more people walking forward was his rationale for having Christians start the ball rolling at altar call time.

This kind of manipulation is an example of the herd instinct. The herding instinct may be defined as a mentality that is characterized by a lack of individual decision making or thoughtfulness, causing people to think and act in the same way as the majority around them. The herd instinct is a major ingredient in the stock market. People may be drawn to a particular stock because they notice others doing the same. They assume it is valuable and don't want to miss out on a good investment. They may not have a clue what the stock is worth, but they reason that if so many people are going that way, it must be a good thing.

It is the bandwagon effect, that people often do or believe what they think many other people do. It is a phenomenon whereby the rate of uptake of beliefs, ideas, facts, and friends increases the more they have already been adopted by others.

In a word: the herd instinct is a case of people not thinking for themselves.

So that is why I ask: why do you think you are a Christian?

We Are All Like Sheep

Douglas MacMillan, a Scottish preacher during the late twentieth century, was a shepherd in the Scottish highlands for years before he entered the ministry. I used to consult him for information about sheep when I was anticipating preaching from certain verses. For example, "The Lord is my shepherd; I shall not want" (Ps. 23:1) and Isaiah 53:6: "All of us like sheep have gone astray; each of us has turned to his own way." Douglas emphasized the herding instinct of sheep, how they always think that the grass is greener on the other side of the fence. "They all club together," he would say. But when Isaiah says that "all of us like sheep have gone astray," it is a humbling reminder that we *all* are guilty of the herding instinct, the club instinct, following the bandwagon.

Its root is in peer pressure, the need to seek approval from our peers. This brings us to that which I call my life verse—John 5:44—which explains the chief reason the Jews rejected their Messiah. Jesus asked: "How can you believe, who receive glory from one another and do not seek the glory that comes from the only God?" I love the New Living Translation (NLT): "No wonder you can't believe! For you gladly honor each other, but you don't care about the honor that comes from the one who alone is God." Or consider the Amplified Bible, Classic Edition (AMPC): "How is it possible for you to believe [how can you learn to believe], you who [are content to seek and] receive praise and honor and glory from one another, and yet do not seek the praise and honor and glory which come from Him Who alone is God?"

It was the herding instinct that led to Jesus's crucifixion. It was the herding instinct that partly lay behind the crowds that followed Jesus. Of the five thousand who followed Jesus and who were fed from five loaves of bread and two fish, Jesus said: "You seek Me not because you saw signs, but because you ate of the loaves and were filled" (John 6:26). When Jesus began to preach things His disciples called "hard sayings," many of them turned back and no longer followed Him (John 6:60, 66). Later on the herding instinct set in and the majority ruled. "Then all the people answered [Pilate the Roman governor], 'His blood be on us and on our children!'" (Matt. 27:25). Among the saddest words in the New Testament are these: "Their shouts prevailed" (Luke 23:23, NIV).

The herding instinct is not what brings a person to the

saving knowledge of Jesus Christ. This is pigeon religion. Those five eight-year-old girls who together responded to the preacher's altar call may have been sincere. But unless *each* of them was individually convicted and persuaded, they were not changed. Hundreds going forward at an evangelistic campaign may be sincere, but unless each one is personally convicted and granted faith and repentance, none of them is converted.

Conversion to Jesus Christ comes from an *individual, personal* decision.

There will be no herding instinct in play at the judgment seat of Christ. No one will be looking at another and saying, "Shall we altogether agree to stand before the judgment seat of Christ?" No. All will be summoned and *made to stand* before the Lord Jesus Christ.

These things said, we all need fellowship. One of the main things that characterized the earliest church was fellowship. It is the second thing Luke mentions following Peter's sermon and the three thousand baptisms on the Day of Pentecost: "They continued steadfastly in (1) the apostles' teaching and (2) fellowship, (3) in the breaking of bread and (4) in the prayers" (Acts 2:42). Fellowship was vital and continues to be essential to our growth. The writer of Hebrews urged early Christian Jews not to forsake the assembling of themselves together (Heb. 10:25). But such fellowship had one thing in common: each of them had decided individually and personally to the call of the gospel.

Conversion is the sovereign work of the Holy Spirit. "The wind blows where it wishes," said Jesus. "You hear its sound, but you do not know where it comes from or where it goes. So it is with *everyone* who is born of the Spirit" (John 3:8, emphasis added).

THE FIRST ALTAR CALL AT WESTMINSTER CHAPEL

When I first invited Arthur Blessitt to speak at Westminster Chapel, the place was packed from top to bottom. Arthur gave what was almost certainly the first altar call at Westminster Chapel. Just before that service, in the vestry (pastor's office) Arthur casually said to me, "Now when I give the invitation..."

I interrupted, "Arthur, we don't do that here."

"We don't?" he replied.

Seeing the look on his face, I said, "Well, if you feel led, go ahead."

I do not question that God can use a crooked stick to draw a straight line.

"I can tell you right now, I do," he quickly answered. He did. It was a daring, courageous thing to do. Having preached for about an hour, he said, "Those who want to receive Jesus, stand up." That was it. There was no singing. None. He just said, "Stand up." To my amazement several stood out of a crowd of at least fifteen hundred.

A woman stood first—all by herself. Years later that woman became my secretary at Westminster Chapel. In that same service was a young man who stood against the protest of his girlfriend next to him. She was very upset that he stood, and he knew it. But he stood anyway. If there was any herd instinct at work that night Arthur preached, one could not tell it. It was a pivotal service in the history of Westminster Chapel.

But cannot God use the herding instinct to bring people to the Lord Jesus? Yes. I do not question that God can use a crooked stick to draw a straight line. "Nothing succeeds like success." Those carried along by the bandwagon effect may nonetheless come to Christ. Furthermore, those disciples in Scripture who went back and stopped following Jesus may well have been truly converted by the Holy Spirit *later*. They heard the Word, and sometimes the Word we hear is like a seed that later comes to fruition.

> *Entertainment will bring crowds. I am for that as long as the gospel—that Jesus's death on the cross is the way of salvation, that His blood is what turns God's wrath away—is preached.*

As I said above, the herding instinct works in finances and sales. I used to sell vacuum cleaners door to door. It helped when I said, "Your friend John Smith just bought one from me." I took full advantage of the herding instinct as a salesman. A friend of mine, noting my success as a salesman, asked me, "Why, RT, don't you use this technique when you are preaching?" I replied, "It is because only the Holy Spirit converts people. I could perhaps get them down to the altar, but that does not mean the Holy Spirit is at work."

The herding instinct is good to get people interested in church. This way they will hopefully hear the gospel. But when it comes to *coming to Christ*, such is the work of the Holy Spirit.

I'm afraid that it is a faulty theology in many places that leads people to think that crowds prove that God is at work. Entertainment will bring crowds. I am for that as long as the gospel—that Jesus's death on the cross is the way of salvation, that His blood is what turns God's wrath away—is preached. The Holy Spirit is essential to a person's true conversion.

When Paul envisaged going to Corinth, he determined to know *nothing* among them but Jesus Christ and Him crucified (1 Cor. 2:2). Why? Isn't this putting Christianity's "worst face forward"—talking about the Son of God being "crucified"? Doesn't Paul know that the Greeks assumed that a person who was crucified was the worst possible criminal and deserved such a punishment? This would surely turn the Greco-Roman mind away from the gospel. Wrong. The Holy Spirit only works when the true gospel is preached, namely, that Jesus died as a propitiation for our sins. That means God's justice was *satisfied* by Jesus's blood. That message is what the Holy Spirit uses to convict lost men and women.

The Heart of the Gospel

I quoted above from Isaiah 53:6. You might like to know that this verse is in what is arguably the greatest Messianic chapter in the Old Testament. You should also know that this verse describes what J. I. Packer calls the *heart of the gospel.* The verse reads: "All of us like sheep have gone astray; each of us has turned to his own way, *but the* Lord *has laid on him the iniquity of us all*" (emphasis added). This verse means that (1) we all are like sheep, who club together; (2) we all have sinned and have come short of the glory of God (Rom. 3:23); and (3) God laid on Jesus all our sins.

The moment we transfer our trust in good works to what Jesus did for us on the cross, a wonderful transaction takes place: our sins are removed and Christ's righteousness comes in. The righteousness is "credited" to us (Rom. 4:5). All that Jesus did for us in His life (keeping the Law for us) and in His death (satisfying God's justice for us) is put to our credit. Those who have this hope are those who will go to heaven and not to hell when they die.

Here is the problem today, generally speaking. Many people come forward in an altar call when there was no gospel preached at all! Those who have a faulty theology hastily assume that all those people were saved! But could not some of them be saved? Yes, because they have hearts after God (owing to the Holy Spirit at work in their lives) and will respond to *any* truth that is preached. But it has been my personal experience, more so in my years of retirement (during which I have preached all over the world), that many, many people have no assurance of salvation but are active in church. The good news is, when many of these people hear the gospel, they respond to it quickly!

Crowds at evangelistic rallies, numbers in churches, and dozens of people showing an interest in religion do not necessarily prove that the Holy Spirit has been at work. There could be a *natural* explanation for hundreds thronging to church. As five thousand people followed Jesus not because of the demonstration of the Spirit's power but because they got their tummies filled, so people can throng to churches because of the natural instinct in all of us not to miss out on what many are doing.

IMPLICIT FAITH

I have to admit that the gospel of Jesus Christ as I understand it today was not faithfully preached at my old church in Ashland, Kentucky. And yet I was sufficiently convicted of my sins that I told my parents *at home* one Easter Sunday morning (April 5, 1942) that I wanted to be saved.

> *Crowds at evangelistic rallies, numbers in churches, and dozens of people showing an interest in religion do not necessarily prove that the Holy Spirit has been at work.*

Some might say: How could *anyone* be saved without hearing the total, undiluted, and historic gospel of Christ? I reply: by what John Calvin calls "implicit faith." That is a term he used for people who had true faith but still lacked a complete knowledge of the gospel. He cites the woman of Samaria in John 4 as being an example of implicit faith. Jesus talked to her, and she became convinced He was the Messiah. But she had an incomplete knowledge of what it means to be saved. She was nonetheless faithful in that which is "least" (Luke 16:10). Calvin not only regarded her as having true faith but added that *all of us* have but an implicit faith since none of us knows everything that is true.

This explains how someone like me could be truly saved having grown up in a church that lacked the teaching I now preach all over the world. We had implicit faith. This means that we believed what we heard. God can use any part of the teaching of the New Testament to bring a person to saving faith. In my boyhood days I knew nothing of the meaning of "propitiation," for example. I do now, and certainly mention it when I preach the gospel.

But it would be unfair to say that a person needs to know profounder truths of the gospel in order to be saved. It would also be easy to describe much of what I experienced in my church in Ashland as pigeon religion, especially compared to what I know now. The truth is, only the Holy Spirit can impart implicit faith. The Holy Spirit was at work when Jesus talked to the woman of Samaria, and the Holy Spirit was at work in the preaching of the pastors and evangelists at my old church in Kentucky.

These things said, reader, do *you* know for certain that if you were to die today you would go to heaven? Do you? And if you were to stand before God (and you will) and He were to say to you (He might), "Why should I let you in to My heaven?" what would your answer be? Let me caution you, at the judgment seat of Christ you will have no one to spoon-feed you the answer. You will have no one nearby to coach you and give you the right answer. You will stand *alone* before the judgment seat of Christ. So will I.

So what comes to your mind right now—what would your answer be to the question, "Why God should let you in to His heaven?"

What about these answers: "I have done my best." "I have tried to live a good life." "I was brought up in a Christian home." "I have lived by the Ten Commandments." "I was baptized." "I love people and try to help them." "I believe in God." Really? So does the devil (James 2:19)!

I must say lovingly but firmly to you, if it did not cross your mind to say: "Because Jesus died for me on the cross"— or the equivalent of that, I would not want to be in your shoes for anything in the world. Unless your hope of heaven is the blood of Jesus, I would urge you to pray this prayer:

> *Lord Jesus Christ, I need You. I want You. I am*
> *sorry for my sins. Thank You for dying on the cross*
> *for my sins. Wash my sins away by Your blood. I*
> *welcome Your Holy Spirit into my heart. As best*
> *as I know how, I give You my life. Amen.*

If you prayed that prayer—and meant it in your heart of hearts—you are born again. You are the work of the sovereign Spirit. If you have never prayed a prayer like that until now, I say: Happy Birthday! Tell at least one other person that you prayed this prayer. Why? Because Jesus said you need to confess Him before others (Matt. 10:32). The person you tell this to may not applaud your decision. If so, it is proof that you may be alone in your commitment to Jesus Christ. Find a church where the Bible is faithfully taught and the gospel as I have briefly explained it in this chapter is preached. God will have a fellowship of people for you. Find your true friends, not those in the world who will not be around at the judgment seat of Christ.

Pigeon religion will always attempt to get into the picture. As I said earlier, there are pigeons at Dove Key in Florida and there are doves in Pigeon Key. But if we get to know the ways of the heavenly Dove, we will be able to detect a pigeon and not be carried along by the crowds.

Yesterday (as it happens) I attended the Wilson County Fair here in Tennessee. I asked my son-in-law Rex to take my picture by a cage in which was a beautiful white pigeon.

While I stood there, a man remarked, "That sure is a wonderful lookin' dove."

I told him, "It's a pigeon."

"Really?" He didn't believe me until he looked at the official label on the cage.

I thought that pigeon was a dove too—until I found out I was wrong. I would hope, however, that one benefit from reading this book will be that we want the genuine Spirit of God to be our Guide. That we will know His ways so well that we will not be deceived by the counterfeit.

Perhaps as a Christian you feel you truly needed this chapter. Is it possible also that you, like a straying sheep, have wandered from "the love you had at first," as the church at Ephesus had done (Rev. 2:4)?

> Return, O holy Dove, return,
> Sweet messenger of rest!
> I hate the sins that made Thee mourn
> And drove Thee from my breast.[1]
> —William Cowper (1731–1800)

Chapter 8

PLAYING THE GAME

He will bring to light what is hidden in darkness and will expose the
motives of the heart. At that time each will receive their praise from God.
—1 CORINTHIANS 4:5, NIV

———— ◆ ————

A pigeon can be trained, domesticated.
A dove cannot be trained.

———

P ETE CANTRELL, TO whom this book is dedicated, told
me that he could put a red box in the center of New
York City and train a pigeon to come to that box.
One of the characteristics of pigeon religion is that people
can be coaxed to do what they believe to be the leading of
the Holy Spirit but which in fact can be the result of their
being manipulated. It can come from hype—intense public
promotion—whether in worship, evangelism, or in a healing
campaign. A well-known worship leader told me how easy it
is to work up a crowd to respond with loud and long praise
to God. One might counter that the Lord could use this to
get people to worship Him—something they ought to do in
any case. Perhaps. Some faith healers have also used this
technique to create an expectancy in those who need healing.
Could not the Lord use this? Perhaps. A powerful evangelist can use tear-jerking illustrations to get people to walk
forward to give their lives to God. Cannot God use a gift of

oratory to persuade people to do what is essentially right to do? Perhaps.

Some Reformed ministers have rejected giving altar calls lest they usurp the ministry of the Holy Spirit. After all, people cannot be converted unless the Holy Spirit draws them (John 6:44). I came under criticism when I began calling people forward at the close of my gospel preaching at Westminster Chapel. My reply is, I never use pressure, but merely give an opportunity for people to do what they want to do—not what they *don't* want to do. When Dr. Martyn Lloyd-Jones preached for me at my Southern Baptist Church in Lower Heyford, Oxfordshire (1974–76), I always stood up afterward and invited people to walk forward in response to his preaching. He would say to me as we drove home, "The way you do that—I have no problem with that at all." I always felt that he would approve of the way I gave appeals at Westminster Chapel.

That said, there have been multitudinous abuses when it comes to high-powered evangelists giving altar calls when dozens and dozens flock to the front but whom you never hear about weeks later.

THE FOLLY OF IMITATING OTHERS

One of the most common occurrences of pigeon religion is how people imitate others. Young preachers often imitate their mentors. But those who do the imitating never capture their hero's genius. God wants each of us to be ourselves. One of the funniest stories I have ever heard was how so many preachers in Great Britain sought to imitate the great Dr. Martyn Lloyd-Jones. Apart from his greatness as a preacher and Bible expositor, Dr. Lloyd-Jones was a bit of an eccentric. I never, ever saw him unless he was wearing a three-piece suit, usually gray, and with a white shirt and tie. He even wore a three-piece suit when going to the beach! While his grandchildren played, there was Dr.

Lloyd-Jones reading the Puritan John Owen in his three-piece suit at the beach! And, would you believe it—yes, some Welsh ministers took to wearing three-piece suits when they went to the beach!

Pigeon religion is inherent in all humankind. Yes, it is in you and it is in me. The theological name is original sin.

Another story—this being told to me by Dr. Lloyd-Jones himself—was how young Welsh preachers sought to imitate an older minister who had an eccentric habit of shaking his hair back. When the hair would get in his face, the preacher—instead of pushing the hair back with his hand—would shake his head so that the hair would go back without using his hand. Consequently, young men all over south Wales would preach and do the same thing—shaking their heads as they preached. One of them was bald-headed, and he too shook his head!

"There's a sucker born every minute" is a phrase often attributed to American showman P. T. Barnum. It means that many people are gullible and we can expect this to continue. People with leadership skills can so easily take advantage of people who are prone to believe almost anything if that leader is loaded with a lot of charisma. Pigeon religion is inherent in all humankind. Yes, it is in you and it is in me. The theological name is *original sin*.

One thing is for certain: you cannot train the Holy Spirit to work! We are totally and eternally dependent on Him to do His work—whether in evangelism, seeing people healed, or in worship. The Spirit will do His work. Our job is to be faithful—preaching the gospel, encouraging people to worship, and praying for the sick.

SPEAKING IN TONGUES

When it comes to the gift of speaking in tongues, there is
the genuine ("Dove religion") and there is the counterfeit
("pigeon religion").

The outpouring of the Holy Spirit at the Azusa Street
Mission in Los Angeles in 1906 gave rise to the largest
Christian movement in church history. No one would have
dreamed back then that the Azusa Street revival—widely criticized by traditional Christians at the time possibly because
of the number of black people involved and certainly because
of the phenomenon of speaking in tongues—would lead to
such vast fame and notoriety. Major denominations such as
the Assemblies of God, the Church of God, and Pentecostal
Holiness—along with the Charismatic Movement, which
began around 1960—have their origin in Azusa Street. This
is to say nothing of third-world Christianity, which is over-
whelmingly Charismatic or Pentecostal. It was an undoubted
move of the fire of God. I have no right to say if pigeon
religion got in (it would be surprising if it didn't), but the
spontaneity—its unplanned nature—and exponential growth
in such a short period of time convinces me that it was one
of the greatest moves of the Spirit since Pentecost.

My old denomination was originally called Pentecostal
Church of the Nazarene (founded in 1908). But speaking in
tongues was not allowed—to put it mildly. Nazarenes had
their roots in the teaching of John Wesley. Their understanding of the baptism with the Holy Spirit was entire sanctification, not speaking in tongues. But because the name
Pentecostal became synonymous with tongues speaking,
the Nazarenes dropped the word Pentecostal from their
name in 1919. As a consequence of this history, I grew up
with an innate prejudice against speaking in tongues. Some
Nazarene leaders even said it was of the devil. So imagine my
own surprise when—in February 1956—driving in my car I
felt a spring inside me wanting to "well up." The only way to

let it out was to utter what I would call unintelligible sounds! I spoke in tongues on my own that day. It came totally unexpectedly and surprisingly, but also embarrassingly, as there were people in the car with me! But I knew I had just spoken in tongues and kept it to myself for a long time.

As my friend Charles Carrin says, speaking in tongues is the only gift of the Spirit that challenges our pride.

When I was pastor of a small church in Carlisle, Ohio, for eighteen months (1962–63), I received a notice that a well-known minister was coming to Middletown, a town nearby. I had read of this man in *Time* magazine a few days before. He was a leader in the "glossolalia" movement (as it was called then), the word taken from the Greek word *glossa*—tongue. Speaking in tongues was breaking out in non-Pentecostal churches all over America, including Episcopal, Reformed, Lutheran, Baptist, and others. I decided to go along to hear this man. As it happened we sat directly across the table from each other at lunch. He told me he was a Calvinist, a minister of the Reformed Church of America. This made me feel safe with him. He gave a brief message, then spoke in tongues for us all. He invited ministers who would like to be prayed for to stay behind. I did.

I knelt at the altar of the church as he laid his hands on me. I had told him that I spoke in tongues—in 1956—but only once. He said this meant I could easily do it again. I was willing to do it again, but I needed to be convinced that God was behind it happening again. When it happened the first time, it came without my seeking it; I wasn't even dreaming of such a thing. But I was willing for this man—who seemed credible—to pray for me that it continue. "Examine all things. Firmly hold onto what is good" (1 Thess. 5:21). As he prayed aloud, I prayed in my heart: "Lord, if this is of You, let it come; if not, stop it."

When he prayed nothing happened. He said, "Well?" I said, "Well?" He then asked me to take the scripture literally: "Make a joyful noise unto the Lord."

"I don't understand," I said.

"Just make a joyful noise," he replied. "Just make a joyful noise."

I was beginning to feel uncomfortable.

"Just make a noise. Say 'Ah.'"

I said "Ah," but by now he had lost me.

"Look, Brother Kendall," he said lovingly to me. "Before Jesus turned the water into wine, He had to have a vessel."

"I am surely that vessel. You've got me on my knees. What more can I do?"

He tried it again. "Just say 'Ah.'"

"'Ah,'" I said. But nothing happened.

I ran into him the next day in a local restaurant. He said he had been praying for me, and added: "That has always worked before."

I believe him. I'm sure it worked before. But could it not have been a number of people playing the game? Possibly. Why didn't it work for me? Probably because I expected it to happen passively as it did the first time. Perhaps I was being unfair. But neither was I ready for that then.

I need to tell you, this was a good man. Now in heaven, he became well known as one of the patriarchs of the Charismatic Movement. I never ran into him again. I think too, as I indicated in *Holy Fire*, that sometimes God uses the very method that same man used with me to bring others to a heavenly language gift. You might make a case that it was sheer pigeon religion. I would have said so at the time. But as I look back on this I think I was being more fearful than spiritual.

I HOPED I WOULD FALL DOWN

Years later, after the Toronto Blessing came on the scene, I queued up in a long line of perhaps fifty ministers—side by side—in an auditorium in London. As it happened I was right in the middle of the line that went from one end of the auditorium to the other. I noticed that every single person fell backward when prayed for. Then the well-known leader (a friend) came to me. I would have *loved* it had the power of God knocked me down. I stood there like the Statue of Liberty. He then said, "God, get this man and I will travel the globe for You"—which made me laugh. But nothing happened. And yet I believe this is a true man of God.

It is so easy for pigeon religion to move in on an authentic move of the Holy Spirit. It would be a mistake to conclude that pigeon religion nullifies the validity of a minister or a move of the Holy Spirit. What often happens is this: God moves sovereignly and powerfully, but not *all* are affected the same way. But those who pray for people sometimes feel a need to make it keep happening. Some even start giving people a little nudge, if not pushing them over. Not good. Pigeon religion.

It happens with the prophetic ministry. I have learned to *never* ask a prophetic person for a "word." They will often give you one! But when you have to ask in order to get their word, there will always be a doubt whether it came from the Lord. Rule of thumb: when you ask a prophetic person for a word, chances are you are unwittingly inviting the pigeon to swoop down rather than the Dove.

One of the greatest evangelists of all time, George Whitefield, fell into this trap in his day. I don't know why he did it—it was so unnecessary (especially for him)—but he had a trumpeter stationed over a hill out of sight, ready to play on signal. He was preaching on the Second Coming, when Gabriel blows the silver trumpet to announce the coming of the Lord. Upon signal, when Whitefield shouted, "Gabriel, don't blow that trumpet," the trumpet sounded not far away. People shrieked and fell to the ground. Pigeon religion. So unnecessary. Whitefield had seen the mighty power of God hundreds of times. Why do this? I'm not sure. But it serves as an example that even the best of us might be tempted to extend a momentum in case the anointing should wane.

Rule of thumb: when you ask a prophetic person for a word, chances are you are unwittingly inviting the pigeon to swoop down rather than the Dove.

For a good number of years there was undoubtedly a touch of God on my old Nazarene church in Ashland, Kentucky. Some of the pastors were among my mentors, and they shaped my thinking and preaching. I have come to the conclusion in recent years that we were possibly the tail end of the momentum that was produced by the Cane Ridge Revival (1801), which I will share more about later. It was the atmosphere in which I developed a genuine fear of the Lord. It was the era in which I was converted. Our church somehow managed to get the best of the Nazarene evangelists when we would annually have three "revivals"—usually lasting two weeks each—in the autumn, winter, and spring.

PIGEON RELIGION AT ITS WORST

A memory of a service at my old church in Ashland stands out. I was sixteen years old. The visiting evangelist had a way of getting people to the altar. The altar was a wooden rail in the front that extended from one side of the church to the other where people could kneel. At the end of his sermon, the visiting evangelist asked everyone to stand. It was a packed church filled with at least five hundred people. When all were standing the evangelist said: "If you know for sure that if you were to die right now you would go straight to heaven and not to hell, please sit down—*But wait!*" the evangelist added. "Don't sit down unless you know beyond a shadow of a doubt that there is nothing between you and God, and that you would go straight to heaven if you died right now. If you know this absolutely, please sit down—*Wait! Don't sit down!*" the preacher warned us. "Remember Ananias and Sapphira, who lied to the Holy Ghost and were struck dead for their lying. Now if you *know* you would go to heaven right now, do please sit down."

Only half of the congregation sat down. By this time the rest were scared to death. He urged those standing to leave their seats and come to the front to get right with God. There wasn't room for them all, but they all tried to get to the altar to kneel and pray.

That service was regarded by many as a great moment— when over a hundred souls tried to make their way to the altar to pray. It was assumed that the Holy Spirit came down in power. I don't think so. I probably thought it then, but it is clear to me now it was pigeon religion. Sadly, it was believed that if you went to the altar, you were sure to get right with God. It did not cross our minds that human manipulation— not the Holy Spirit—is what got people to go forward.

THE BROWNSVILLE REVIVAL

Some readers will recall the Brownsville revival in Pensacola, Florida (from June 18, 1995 to 2000). Louise and I attended it. One had to arrive early; some actually came thirteen hours before the service to be sure they got seated inside. I will never forget the long lines. I also noticed a huge sign out in front of the church—changed daily—noting the number of "salvations" that occurred since the revival started a year or so before: 54,231. That is an impressive number for a series of meetings that only began a year or so before. That still gave me pause. Why did they need to hype it when it was still going on? When we finally got seated—an hour before the worship began—we could feel how the atmosphere was charged with expectancy. The evangelist preached one of the greatest expositions from the Book of Joshua I ever heard. So far, so good. But when he came to his altar call, he threw in the following: "If you have watched an R-rated movie in the last six weeks, if you have drunk a Budweiser in the last six weeks, if you have looked at a Victoria's Secret catalogue (that shows women dressed in very sensual lingerie) in the previous six weeks, you need to hit this altar *now*." People by the hundreds got up from the pews spontaneously and *ran* to the front. They did not walk. They ran. But I also found out that some of these same people had run to the front a number of times before. And when they signed the card for why they came forward, they apparently claimed to be getting "saved." Some were baptized and rebaptized. That is partly how the numbers went so high in a short period of time. This is because of the *people's* theological background. It would seem that many who went forward had an understanding of salvation that taught them that if they drank a bottle of beer or looked at a Victoria's Secret catalogue their salvation was canceled. So they felt they had to go to the altar again and get saved again.

However, owing to the influence of theologian Dr. Michael Brown, the Brownsville people stopped changing the daily number of "salvations" on the sign in front of the church. Furthermore, it was not the Brownsville theology that purported that people lost their salvation if they drank a Budweiser. The evangelist only urged people to come to the altar to get right with God "if they were playing games with sin, had drifted from the Lord, or never knew Him," as Dr. Brown put it. People who had very sensitive consciences and feared they were not right with God would feel that they needed to come to the altar again. I can sympathize with this. This sounds like me when I was a teenager in my Nazarene church! In any case, a database was kept and people's names were entered only once. Over 300,000 different people responded to the altar calls during the Brownsville revival. Over four million people attended the revival. By any calculation, that is amazing. But as Dr. Michael Brown put it, "How many were first time converts, only God knows."

I believe that the Brownsville Revival was—generally—a powerful move of the Holy Spirit. It was not all pigeon religion. But some of it was—as in any revival. It is sad, however, when a faulty theology governs people's thinking and keeps them from trusting the finished work of Jesus Christ on the cross. Salvation is by grace through faith and not of works (Eph. 2:8–9).

Pigeon religion is never far away when the genuine Holy Spirit is powerfully at work.

The Brownsville Revival eventually waned. All anointings of the Spirit come and go. Only with Jesus did the dove come down and *remain* (John 1:32–33). This is because Jesus never—ever—grieved the Holy Spirit. But for the rest of us, like it or not, the Dove does not remain on us but flies away. Keep in mind this is a metaphor. For the Holy Spirit never leaves us. We do, however, at times forfeit the sense of His presence.

That is what happened in the 1950s—the era of undoubted healing revivals. There is *no doubt* that thousands were miraculously healed during that decade. But God is sovereign. For reasons known only to Him, the anointing began to lift and fewer and fewer people were healed. Then it came to a trickle. But some of these evangelists—by this time buying time on television—needed to keep it going.

Another Pentecostal statesman (a man I respected, especially after I got to know him) is an example. His emphasis shifted from miraculous healing to other things. He eventually made (in my opinion) some foolish comments; he would be the first to agree. I knew he would welcome the chance to write the foreword to my book *How to Forgive Ourselves Totally.* It would be a mistake to dismiss his entire ministry as pigeon religion just because of mistakes he made.

We have all done this. Pigeon religion is never far away when the genuine Holy Spirit is powerfully at work. Sometimes even in the midst of God powerfully working there is the possibility of pigeon religion.

PIGEON RELIGION AT JESUS'S TRANSFIGURATION

Consider the transfiguration of Jesus. This has to be one of the most extraordinary manifestations of the glory of God in either the Old or New Testament. One would have thought that there is *surely no possibility* that pigeon religion would slip in. But it did. Jesus had taken Peter, James, and John to a high mountain. Suddenly Jesus was transfigured before them. "His face shone as the sun, and His garments became as white as the light" (Matt. 17:2). Then Moses and Elijah appeared before them, talking with Jesus.

Enter pigeon religion: "Peter said to Jesus, 'Lord, it is good for us to be here. If you wish, I will put up three shelters—one for you, one for Moses and one for Elijah'" (Matt. 17:4, NIV). What an inane, silly, and foolish comment! One would think that the presence of God was so strong that it would be impossible for the flesh to get in. But it did.

This goes to show how the flesh gets in so easily, even with the most sincere people. At the height of the Toronto Blessing, some people were taking buckets to Toronto. They hoped to bring the Holy Spirit back to their churches in these buckets. This sort of thing gives critics an opportunity to laugh their heads off—and I don't mean the kind of laughter they were experiencing at Toronto Airport Christian Fellowship. If only we could put the Holy Spirit in a bucket—and then pour it on people to see them helped or healed! If only. But the Holy Spirit—like the wind—will do what He wills to do (John 3:8). He is sovereign. We cannot manipulate him to do what we wish He would do. You can train a pigeon, but you cannot train a dove.

IS THE HOLY SPIRIT A GENTLEMAN?

While I was finishing this very book there came news that a Scottish self-proclaimed prophet walked onto the platform of a well-known evangelical minister while this minister was preaching. The so-called prophet said that God told him to warn this minister regarding his cessationist teaching. The question is, could God have truly sent this man to interrupt the service like that? I am personally embarrassed by this incident, and it does the reputation of noncessationist Reformed people (namely, charismatics and Pentecostals) no good. But could God have been behind this? I would agree with what the man said but not how and where he said it. That is my opinion. But what if God would use this man to embarrass me too? So *could* God have sent this Scot to warn the famous evangelical? Perhaps. As C. S. Lewis wrote of Aslan the lion in The Chronicles of Narnia: he is "good" but may not be "safe."

A pivotal service in my own personal pilgrimage took place in my old church in Ashland in April 1956. Services were being held every evening. A group of men decided to stay in the church after the service one evening and hold an all-night prayer meeting. They prayed into the early hours of the morning and much of the following day. In the church service the following evening, one of those men suddenly interrupted the congregational singing. They were singing the hymn "The Unclouded Day"; the organist stopped playing. This man walked up and down the aisles of the church, shouting, "Someone here is holding up the revival. I know his name. I love this man. Ichabod is written over the door of this church." Some of the people felt it was a warning from God; some were convinced it was of the flesh. I believe it was of God. As a consequence of my opinion on this service, my life was never to be the same again. And yet if indeed this was the Holy Spirit at work, He hardly seemed like a gentleman.

There are two other things worth mentioning about the Ashland service. A haze came over the congregation while the man exhorted. It was present for a few moments. It reminded one of the smoke—or cloud—in the temple in Old Testament times (2 Chron. 5:13; Ezek. 10:3). If this cloud was truly a visible manifestation of the presence of God, it was surely a seal of God on the service and the way it was proceeding. The second thing is this: There is good reason to think that Ichabod *was* written over my old church. Ichabod means "the glory has departed." That church was never the same again after then. The old spirit apparently completely diminished in that place. Attendance dwindled. What was once regarded as a leading, powerful church in the denomination became less than mediocre in a very short period of time.

For what it's worth, I told the above story—but in more detail—to Dr. Martyn Lloyd-Jones. I was apprehensive as to what his reaction might be. I therefore told the same story to him again, two years later. Both times he affirmed that the unusual service was a manifestation of the Holy Spirit in which God was indeed speaking to someone present who needed it.

Following the way of the Holy Spirit comes with great cost. It almost always means going against fear and pride. But the cost is worth it.

Is the Holy Spirit a gentleman? My answer: sometimes. But not always. As we saw in chapter 1, never forget how Uzzah reached out to steady the ark of God with his hand when the oxen that carried it stumbled. What Uzzah did seemed so appropriate and innocent. But "the LORD became angry against Uzzah, and God struck him down on the spot for his irreverence. He died there beside the ark of God" (2 Sam. 6:7). Now read the account of how Ananias and Sapphira lied to the Holy Spirit and were struck dead instantly before all in Acts 5:1–11.

As William Cowper put it, "God moves in a mysterious way His wonders to perform."[1] The Holy Spirit can at times make us very, very uncomfortable.

Playing the game is usually the easy thing to do. I have

written this book to warn all of us that we must stop playing the game and be willing to go outside our comfort zones. Following the way of the Holy Spirit comes with great cost. It almost always means going against fear and pride. But the cost is worth it. For the presence of the mind of the Spirit is the ultimate wisdom. Though it cost you all you have, don't stop short of true understanding (Prov. 4:7).

One of the most encouraging things I have heard lately comes from Bobby Conner. I have heard him say it several times: "The fear of the Lord is coming back to the church." May it come soon.

Chapter 9

MY OWN PIGEON RELIGION

*Are you so foolish? Having begun by the Spirit, are
you now being perfected by the flesh?*
—GALATIANS 3:3, ESV

———— ◆ ————

**Pigeons take themselves very seriously.
Doves do not take themselves seriously.**

————

HAVE YOU THOUGHT that I am exposing pigeon religion in every place on the planet but in myself? As
the saying goes, "It takes one to know one." Indeed,
one person's traits are most quickly recognized by another
person who shares those same traits. Jesus told us not to
judge so that we would not be judged (Matt. 7:1).

I will try my best to come clean and be very candid. I
could well be the supreme example of pigeon religion. I continually marvel that God would use me. If you really knew
me, you would become convinced that God can use anybody!

One of my favorite fishing spots is near Dove Key, a small
island in the Florida Keys just offshore from Key Largo. The
truth is, I have seen more pigeons there than doves! Further
south in the Florida Keys is Pigeon Key (near the Seven Mile
Bridge). I am sure that doves frequent that little island too.

The truth is, we are all a mixed bag. I wish that I were so
spiritual that I had no pigeon religion in me. If only!

My friend Lyndon Bowring prays for me every day (at my request) that I will not take myself so seriously. As I said above, this is almost certainly one of my greatest weaknesses. Taking oneself too seriously comes from original sin, of course, but is enhanced in my case, I think, by at least three other things: (1) I was an only child until my little sister was born when I was fifteen. I therefore have the personality of an only child. My parents doted on me, and part of the result of this has been a driving ambition to succeed; (2) my church background, which has possibly contributed to my striving for perfection; and (3) authentic experiences from the Holy Spirit, some of which I may have misinterpreted or augmented to suit my personal wishes.

You may recall that my dad named me after his favorite preacher, Dr. R. T. Williams, general superintendent of the Church of the Nazarene. I had godly parents. My first memory of my dad was seeing him on his knees, praying for thirty minutes (alongside reading his Bible) before going to work each day. My earliest memory of my mother was similar: seeing her on her knees with her hands lifted to heaven as she prayed every morning after my dad went to work. I was converted at the age of six, kneeling at my parents' bedside on Easter morning, April 5, 1942.

I treasure my Nazarene heritage. Dr. Martyn Lloyd-Jones used to say to me again and again, "Don't forget your Nazarene background; it is what has saved you" (from being a cold orthodox theologian). I agree. I have spoken well of my Nazarene background all over the world. Nazarenes in Britain know of my fondness for them and my background. Trevecca Nazarene University awarded me with a doctor of divinity degree in 2007.

Very Strict Upbringing

Although I believe I was truly converted at the age of six, I struggled to know whether I was "sanctified wholly." As far back as I can remember—and even to this day—I have a problem with my temper. My old denomination put a lot of stress on entire sanctification being the eradication of the carnal nature—including your temper. Nazarenes used to say to me, "God will take that temper away from you if you get sanctified." I did all I knew to do. But I never got to the place where I did not lose my temper.

Nazarene preachers preached the doctrine of "entire sanctification," generally following John Wesley (although Nazarene scholars now debate whether they were true to Wesley). Nazarenes believe in two works of grace: one needs to be "saved" and then "sanctified wholly." The latter supposedly enables one to live "above" sin. Some of their leaders, including my pastors, taught sinless perfection. I was not allowed to go to the cinema, the circus, school dances, to play cards, or wear a class ring. My mother did not wear a wedding ring because 1 Timothy 2:9 forbids the wearing of gold. She might have worn a silver one, but that would indicate the "appearance of evil." I never knew for sure if I was truly saved, since Nazarenes teach you can lose your salvation if you sin. Therefore my conversion was rendered of no value if I sinned. I did not have assurance I would not go to hell. I feared going to hell if I did something wrong. I would do what they said was required in order to be sanctified wholly—putting "my all on the altar." But if I lost my temper (a problem, as I said, I have had all my life), it meant I was not sanctified yet.

MY DEFINING MOMENT

After I entered the Nazarene ministry, I no doubt had a subconscious wish of becoming a leader in my denomination. I was incapable of thinking outside the "Nazarene box." I became a student of Trevecca Nazarene College (now University) in September 1953. During my second year at Trevecca, at the age of nineteen, I felt called to preach.

Three months later I became a student pastor of the Church of the Nazarene in Palmer, Tennessee—preaching there on weekends. During my third year at Trevecca—on October 31, 1955—I was given an experience by the Holy Spirit that would become the defining moment of my life and ministry.

As I was praying while driving back to Trevecca on that Monday morning, there appeared to me the Lord Jesus. Although it was a vision, it was as clear as though I saw Him with my naked eye. He was interceding for me at the Father's right hand. An hour or so later I heard Him say to the Father, "He wants it."

I heard the Father's reply: "He can have it."

I entered into a rest of soul unlike anything I had ever known. The peace was incredible. I knew I was *saved*. Eternally saved. By sundown that day I was given to see that what happened to me was a sovereign work of the Holy Spirit.

In the following months the doctrines of election and pre-destination were supernaturally opened to me—all without reading or hearing a single sermon on those subjects, without reading a word of John Calvin or any Reformed theologian. I will be as honest with you as I know how. There was no pigeon religion at that stage of my life. I had *plerophoria* (full assurance) of salvation, and to some degree, *plerophoria* of understanding. There was a time when I wondered if I had discovered something entirely knew.

During this period I began to have other visions. I never had visions before. I will never forget a vision of me preaching in a famous venue in New York City. Behind me was a choir; all were wearing light blue and silver robes. I have never known whether that was a vision to be taken lit-erally or if it merely pointed to a wider ministry outside my old denomination.

Could I have made up the vision? Would not preaching in a famous venue in New York be exactly what I could wish for? Yes. But for some reason I have never dismissed this as pigeon religion. For one thing, it was the first hint I would not always be a Nazarene. It served as preparation. If it was symbolic—which is possible—it meant a wider ministry for me one day.

However, months later the same vision was repeated, this time showing a lady in the choir who had blonde hair. Enter pigeon religion. I took the vision to mean I would marry a girl with blonde hair. I told all my friends I would marry a blonde someday. But I didn't. Louise had brown hair.

Not marrying a blonde hurt my credibility with my old Trevecca associates. It gave them legitimacy in rejecting not only my visions but my newly found theology as well. I could not blame them. For if I was wrong about the vision concerning the blonde, it surely follows I was wrong about my coming into a different theology. What is more, I have never to this day preached in New York City.

I could make a weak case that the vision was partly fulfilled at a church of which I became the pastor in Fort Lauderdale years later. The robes were like those in the vision, and there was a teenaged girl in the choir with the same blonde hair. But I honestly do not believe the vision was in fact fulfilled. Perhaps it was symbolic. To be totally honest, this vision of me preaching in New York City remains a mystery to me. It also is very humbling. I may never know until I get to heaven why I had that vision.

During those days I also had a vision of my father. He was wearing a light green suit. He walked down the center aisle in a church that had windows on one side but a wall on the other. I had no idea what it meant. Six years later when I was pastor of a church in Carlisle, Ohio, the vision was literally fulfilled.

What was the purpose of this vision? The same church turned against my preaching and sought to throw me out months later. I eventually gave up and resigned the church. The vision, however, gave me peace that I was supposed to be there. It also made me see by direct experience a profound theological truth—that God knows the future as perfectly as He knows the past. There was no pigeon religion in this vision.

THE DANGER WITH VISIONS

It is my experience that, having had perhaps a dozen visions in 1955–56, it is easy to imagine you are having a vision when you are actually making it up. I did this at least once. I was so upset with a particular relative that I allowed myself to think I was seeing something when I wasn't. Pigeon religion. This experience taught me how imagining a vision could happen. I will say that many of those visions have been fulfilled—literally. But some remain a mystery, and some have not been fulfilled.

Pigeon religion entered my life in those days largely because I wanted to convince my dad that I was on the right track. I *so* wanted his approval. He was devastated at the thought of my leaving the Nazarenes and embracing the theology called Calvinism. He would wake up at night weeping over my new direction. This deeply hurt me. In August 1956, in order to make him feel better, I told him of a vision that would absolutely be fulfilled in one year. He said, "Will you put that in writing?" Yes. So I signed my name to a vision that I promised would be fulfilled in twelve months. It wasn't. Pigeon religion. This understandably convinced my father that I was *truly* out of God's will. Not only that; five years later I was working as a door-to-door vacuum cleaner salesman.

In 1978—twenty-two years later—as the train was pulling into London's King's Cross station, I heard actually heard these words from my dad: "Son, I am proud of you. You were right and I was wrong." It took my being the minister of Westminster Chapel to convince him.

Pigeon religion can emerge as an attempt of the flesh to add human efforts to what was initiated by the Holy Spirit. Hence Paul's question to the Galatians who were turning to legalism, "Having begun in the Spirit, are you now being perfected by the flesh?" (Gal. 3:3). Pigeon religion is manifested by running ahead of the Lord, lagging behind, trying to find fulfillment through legalism, or trying to make one-self look good.

The peace that was given to me on that October morning in 1955 lasted for some ten months. Those ten months were so beautiful. During that time I had extraordinary peace: a continual rest of soul and an unusual sense of guidance. Twice a voice within—I truly believe it was the Holy Spirit—directly spoke texts in the Bible when I had no idea what they would say until I turned to them. When I would turn in the Bible to see what the verses were, they gave supernatural assurance I was truly being led by God. As I stated above, in 1956 I spoke in tongues for the first time. This experience was accompanied with supernatural predictions regarding things that should take place weeks later. They did—exactly as I was told. I also wrote several hymns and choruses in those days.

THE DAY I LOST MY PEACE

But in August 1956, pigeon religion wormed its way into my soul. Someone made a totally false and horrible accusa-tion at me. I lost my temper. I also lost that peace. Those ten months of bliss came to a sudden end. I knew immediately that peace was gone. I was so sorry. The accusation was so unfair and untrue, but I grieved the Holy Spirit by losing my temper. God won't bend the rules for any of us. For many years I tried every way in the world to get that peace back.

In 1962 I became the minister of the Fairview Church of God in Carlisle, Ohio. I was largely rejected by the people there. They could not abide my teaching of sovereign grace. I had been assured by my old mentor that "they will believe anything you preach if you can show it to them in the Bible." That did not turn out to be the case. We stayed eighteen months. My old mentor turned his back on me while I was there, resulting in what was arguably the severest trauma of my entire life. Pigeon religion got into my heart big-time. I am ashamed to admit that I carried a deep grudge against this man for many years. There was no peace in my soul for a long, long time. I am amazed that God used me at all during those years. How foolish I was to live in hate and bitterness all those years, but I did.

The peace eventually returned—in stages. But it was not until 1980, when I learned to dignify trials, that I began to experience this peace I had back in 1955–56. This peace came when I was preaching on James 1:2: "Count it all joy when you fall into diverse temptations." The NIV puts it this way: "Consider it pure joy, my brothers and sisters, whenever you face trials of many kinds." As I learned to "dignify" trials, even the most minute and seemingly insignificant trial, that old peace began to come back into my soul. By dignifying trials I mean esteeming them as coming directly from God; not complaining and not trying to end them. All trials have their built-in time limit. They will end. Don't rush through them but find out what God wants to teach you. That is what I mean by dignifying trials. By putting these principles into practice, I personally experienced a true revival in my soul.

Later on, through the previously mentioned influence of Josef Tson, I was compelled to forgive—totally—all who hurt me. That was the time when the peace of those former years fully came back. I was able to forgive my old mentor. Totally. As I state in my book *Total Forgiveness,* the act of total forgiveness is not necessarily reconciliation. And sometimes reconciliation would not be good. But in this case there was a most beautiful reconciliation. And yet this long experience of bitterness taught me a hard lesson: it is much easier to lose the peace of the Dove than it is to get it back.

LEARNING ANOTHER LESSON

During the years 1982–1984, I am ashamed to admit, I sometimes preached "at" those in the Chapel who were opposing my ministry. If you were to listen to the tapes of my sermons on 1 John during those years, you might pick up on this. I am ashamed of it. I became defensive. Even my supporters knew it. Pigeon religion surfaced. That said, whereas on the one hand it was my endeavoring to practice total forgiveness that saved me in those days, on the other hand I said things that violated this teaching. I was out of order to make innuendos and not-very-subtle comments about my opposition. God might so easily have removed me; my supporters might have turned against me. But God was gracious to me and I survived. But hopefully I have never preached "at" people since.

> *All trials have their built-in time limit. They will end. Don't rush through them but find out what God wants to teach you.*

I have had only two visions since 1956. Both came while I was at Westminster Chapel, and both were similar. They remain unfulfilled. In the visions I saw countless people in Westminster Chapel. I took the visions to mean that revival would come to Westminster Chapel. Although we had undoubted touches of the Spirit on us in my last few years at the Chapel, revival did not come. Were those visions pigeon religion? I have no idea.

My greatest sin of those twenty-five years at Westminster Chapel was to take myself too seriously. I could not see it then. I see it now. People who take themselves too seriously cannot laugh at themselves. They become hypersensitive to criticism and fear they won't get credit for the good things they have done. I am so guilty here.

If I could turn the clock back and start all over, I might well avoid many pitfalls—especially not putting my family first as I should have done. I put the church and sermon preparation first, thinking I was putting God first. Wrong. The Dove would have put my family first. The pigeon had me put preaching first and take myself so seriously. I now believe that if I had put my family first I would have preached *just as well*. But I cannot get those years back.

But there is good news. God restores "the years the locusts have eaten" (Joel 2:25). Both of our children are happily married and live very near Louise and me. Only forty-five minutes away, we see them all the time. Our son TR works with me full time—managing my website and books—and travels with me around the world. All things work together for good to them that love God (Rom. 8:28). The fact that all things work together for good does not mean that what happened in the past was right at the time. Rather, the good, the bad, and the ugly sooner or later work together for good. Pigeon religion is defeated in the end. Glory to God.

Chapter 10

THE CANE RIDGE REVIVAL: AMERICA'S SECOND GREAT AWAKENING

Repent, then, and turn to God, so that your sins may be wiped out, that times of refreshing may come from the Lord.

—ACTS 3:19, NIV

———————◆———————

**Pigeons protect their nests.
Doves do not protect their nests.**

———|———

W HY WRITE A chapter that is devoted almost entirely to the Cane Ridge Revival? For two reasons. First, it is because many Christians have never heard of the Cane Ridge Revival. I believe they should know about it. There would have been no "Bible Belt" in the United States had there been no Cane Ridge Revival. Although the Bible Belt may be shallow in places today ("a thousand miles wide and one inch deep," as some would say), we are all the better for the Bible Belt.

Second, although I am identified as a Reformed Charismatic and most of my preaching invitations come from Charismatic churches, I think we all can learn to be a bit more tolerant of those who are not ministering and worshipping in our "territory." Many Charismatics assume that unless the gifts of the Spirit are prominent, the Spirit must not be present. I think that is a hasty assumption. This chapter shows that God can be at work and yet many of the gifts of the Spirit not be so prominent.

THE FIRST GREAT AWAKENING

In 1976, to commemorate the two hundredth anniversary of the Declaration of Independence, at the invitation of Dr. Martyn Lloyd-Jones, I gave the Annual Lecture of the Evangelical Library of London. In it I focused on the influence of America's New England Awakening on the Declaration of Independence. I took the view that the Great Awakening led directly to the formation of the Declaration of Independence in 1776. Dr. Lloyd-Jones stood up afterward and spoke for several minutes, endorsing my perspective.

All American church historians agree that there have been *two* Great Awakenings in the United States. The first is the New England Great Awakening (ca. 1735–1750). The main figures were Jonathan Edwards, George Whitefield, and Gilbert Tennent.

The high-water mark was probably when Jonathan Edwards preached his sermon "Sinners in the Hands of an Angry God" (the title given by the printer when the sermon went to press). At a congregational meeting house in Enfield, Connecticut, on July 8, 1741, taking his text from Deuteronomy 32:35, KJV, "Their foot shall slide in due time," Edwards began to describe the horrors of hell. He read from a manuscript. He stated that it was by the very mercy of God that his hearers were not in hell at that very moment.

As he spoke people began to groan and moan. Edwards asked them to be quiet so he could finish. The consternation of the people was felt so deeply that their agony was vocalized with anxiety. When he finished, some of the people were holding on to church pews to keep from sliding into hell. Men were seen outside the building holding on to tree trunks to keep from sliding into hell. News of the sermon went all over New England in days, all over England in weeks. The term "great awakening" and Edwards's sermon sometimes came to be used almost interchangeably.

Louise and I have made four trips (so far) to Enfield, Connecticut. We go there to stand or kneel and to pray: "Lord, do it again." In a vacant lot across the street from the Montessori school there is a plaque imbedded in the ground. I am told by local residents that many of the people in Enfield are embarrassed by it. The plaque reads:

> This boulder marks the place where stood the Second Meeting House of the First Church of Christ in Enfield. Built A.D. 1704 and used for worship until 1775. In this Meeting House on July 8, 1741, during the revival known as "THE GREAT AWAKENING" Jonathan Edwards preached his celebrated sermon "SINNERS IN THE HANDS OF AN ANGRY GOD."

Edwards preached the sermon again elsewhere two weeks later with no effect whatever. God only did it once. It was just a *taste* of what it is like to experience the wrath of God. No pigeon religion here. This was an authentic outpouring of the Holy Spirit; a seal on the New Testament teaching of eternal punishment. The first message of the New Testament was John the Baptist preaching on how to escape from the wrath of God (Matt. 3:7).

The high-water mark was probably when Jonathan Edwards preached his sermon "Sinners in the Hands of an Angry God."

In England the famous George Whitefield (1714–1770) ceased preaching in pulpits and went to the fields to preach to ordinary people. John Wesley criticized Whitefield for doing this. Not only that; strange manifestations emerged when Whitefield preached: barking, weeping, shouting, laughing, swooning (falling). Wesley told Whitefield in so many words, "You know that much of this is of the flesh." Agreed, said Whitefield. "Then stamp out what is false," said Wesley. Whitefield replied that if you try to stamp out what is false, you will also stamp out what is real. One must leave it. Later Wesley himself took to the fields and witnessed the same manifestations. It is much like the parable of the wheat and tares, or weeds; instead of getting rid of the weeds, they must grow up together (Matt. 13:30).

Part of the stigma of true revival is that the flesh—pigeon religion—somehow gets in. Jonathan Edwards said that when the church is revived, so is the devil!

George Whitefield came to America and became one of the main figures in the Great Awakening. He was arguably the greatest evangelist of all time. But, as I said above, even he sadly let pigeon religion get into his preaching. (I refer to the incident of the trumpet player that I wrote about earlier in this book).

Gilbert Tennent (1703–1764), a friend of Whitefield, was a Presbyterian preacher who also figured largely in the New England Great Awakening. He became famous for his sermon "The Danger of an Unconverted Ministry," which enraged many traditional ministers. He feared that many of them had gone into the preaching ministry but had never been converted. His sermon was harsh. He called many ministers Pharisee teachers. He is blamed for causing a great split among the ministers, especially Presbyterians, in New England. Pigeon religion? There was undoubted truth in Tennent's sermon, although it is said that he later regretted preaching it. Some thought he was getting at one minister in particular. If so, that may well be called pigeon religion.

JAMES MCGREADY (1763–1817) AND THE LOGAN COUNTY REVIVAL

The Rev. James McGready was a strong, fearless frontiersman preacher who was heavily influenced by his Scottish-Irish background. Born in Pennsylvania, he became pastor of a Presbyterian church in North Carolina. But his preaching rubbed people the wrong way, and in 1796 he eventually left, ending up in Logan County, Kentucky, near the Tennessee border forty miles north of Nashville. He took over three small congregations, each named after the Red River, Muddy River, and Gasper River. Although he believed in predestination, he was not controlled by it. McGready was "a combination of Daniel Boone and Billy Graham," writer Stephen Mansfield said to me. He was a rugged preacher who had a burden for the lost but also emphasized holy living—the kind that got him into trouble in North Carolina. I am indebted to Stephen Mansfield for much of the material that relates to the Logan County revival. Shortly after McGready became the minister of the three churches in Kentucky (in 1797), he came up with this Covenant which he asked all the members to sign:

> When we consider the word and promises of a compassionate God, to the poor lost family of Adam, we find the strongest encouragement for Christians to pray in faith—to ask in the name of Jesus for the conversion of their fellow-man. None ever went to Christ when on earth, with the case of their friends, that were denied, and, although the days of his humiliation are ended, yet for the encouragement of his people, he has left it on record, that where two or three agree, upon earth, to ask in prayer, *believing*, it shall be done. Again, *whatsoever you shall ask the Father in my name, that will I do, that the Father may be glorified in the Son*. With these promises

before us, we feel encouraged to unite our suppli-
cation to a prayer hearing God, for the outpouring
of his Spirit, that his people may be quickened and
comforted, and that our children, and sinners generally, may be converted. Therefore, we bind ourselves
to observe the third Saturday of each month, for one
year, as a day of fasting and prayer for the conversion of sinners in Logan County, and throughout
the world. We also engage to spend one half hour
every Saturday evening, beginning at the setting of
the sun, and one half hour every Sabbath morning,
from the rising of the sun, in pleading with God to
revive his work.[1]

In June of 1800 four or five hundred members of the three
congregations met at the Red River meeting house for a
series of services scheduled to last from Friday to Monday, a
five-day Scottish Communion service. It was a time of deep
soul-searching and sometimes agonizing over whether one
was truly converted. Some among them had been praying
for revival for more than three years. Expectation ran high.

For the first few days of the meeting, people were touched
repeatedly. But on the last service of the last day, the dam broke.
William Hodge, a minister who had joined McGready, preached
a long and powerful sermon. People began to weep, and one
woman in the east of the building began to cry and shout.

When Hodge finished his sermon, Methodist preacher
John McGee of the Cumberland Valley strode to the pulpit.
McGee began to sense the power of what was happening and
later reported, "There was one greater than I preaching." As
he continued his sermon:

I exhorted them to let the Lord Omnipotent reign
in their hearts and submit to him, and their souls
should live. Many broke silence. The woman in the
east end of the house shouted tremendously. I left

the pulpit to go to her. Several spoke to me: "You know these people. Presbyterians are much for order, they will not bear this confusion." I turned to go back—and was near falling, the power of God was strong upon me. I turned again and losing sight of fear of man, I went through the house exhorting with all possible ecstasy and energy.[2]

The pandemonium that ensued was overwhelming. Worshippers were overcome by what they thought to be the power of God and fell unconscious to the floor, a condition those in attendance called "slain" because of its deathlike appearance. McGready remembered that the floor was "covered with the slain; their screams for mercy pierced the heavens."

BARTON W. STONE (1772–1844) AND THE CANE RIDGE REVIVAL

What is described above was but the forerunner to what is, by some reckonings, the greatest revival America has ever seen. For the best and most powerful was yet to come. It took place the following year, in 1801, in Bourbon County, Kentucky, just east of Lexington. It took place in an area called Cane Ridge, the name given by Daniel Boone, owing to the abundance of cane growing in the area. After the 1800 revival in Logan County, Kentucky, Barton W. Stone invited people of all denominations to come to Cane Ridge for a time of Bible study and fellowship. He was thus the host pastor of a gathering that had an estimated fifteen to twenty thousand people in attendance. It was to be centered on the Scottish way of administering the Lord's Supper, as in the Logan County meetings. Although the first of the "camp meetings" was in Logan County, Cane Ridge would afterward be the place to which nearly all would refer. No one was prepared for what happened there, as we will see below.

Born in Maryland, Barton W. Stone was brought up in

an upper middle class home. He was christened by a Church of England priest. At the age of eighteen, while a student at Guildford Academy in North Carolina, he heard James McGready preach. He was deeply moved by McGready and was ordained a Presbyterian a few years later. In 1798 he became the pastor of two Presbyterian churches in Bourbon County—Concord and Cane Ridge. According to historian Paul K. Conkin, Stone's forte was organization and ecumenical cooperation. He did not have McGready's pulpit skills. His background "in no wise prepared him for Cane Ridge or gave any hint that he would occupy a strategic position in the great revival, a position that involved circumstances more than talent."[3]

He established close working relationships with Methodists. In 1800 Stone went to visit James McGready after the revival had broken out in the churches in Logan County. Stone suggested that people come to Cane Ridge in 1801, a gathering that would make the Lord's Supper central. People of all denominations were invited. In August 1801, thousands came in their covered wagons from several states, especially Ohio, Virginia, North Carolina, Tennessee, and from all over Kentucky.

During the day on August 6, 1801, people began arriving at Cane Ridge. By Saturday the roads were jammed with hundreds of wagons. People camped on the ground and immediately began praising God day and night. The Cane Ridge congregation had built a large tent about a hundred yards from the meetinghouse (which had a capacity of five hundred with people standing). Whether they also spread straw or arranged log seats is not clear. Members of the congregation brought food and spread it on long tables. But there was not enough food for everyone. Horses needed water twice a day, but the nearest river or stream was a mile away. "One of the mysteries of Cane Ridge is how the people attending procured the water needed even for themselves," said Conkin.[4] This is to say nothing of toilet facilities. Cane Ridge was not prepared for such a gathering. But it seemed that people—at least for a while—forgot about food or sleep.

> *Outside the meeting house people were groaning and falling to the ground. Some fell and were unconscious, others were conscious. A few fell into a deep coma.*

The grounds filled on Saturday. Thousands flooded in from the middle Kentucky area. It was supposed to be a period of preparation. People were to ready themselves spiritually for the coming Communion. But by Saturday afternoon the preaching was continual, from both the meetinghouse and the tent. According to Conkin, "the excitement built, and before dark the grounds echoed penitent cries and shouts punctuated by the crying of babies and the screaming of children and the neighing of horses. When visitors first arrived they were astonished at the sound, the sheer level of noise."[5] It was referred to as "the roar of Niagara," as people could hear it from great distances.

The central purpose of the gathering—the Communion—took place in the meetinghouse on Sunday. A Presbyterian minister preached a traditional sermon outside in the tent. But communicants moved into the meetinghouse for the serving of the bread and wine. The number ranged from eight hundred to seven thousand, although the actual number of those partaking of the Lord's Supper was probably far less than seven thousand. Members of at least ten Presbyterian congregations in central Kentucky actively cooperated in the Communion. Only Presbyterian ministers presided. Methodist ministers apparently felt excluded.

Pigeons protect their nests. The Presbyterians apparently wanted control.

Thirteen Presbyterian ministers either preached or served tables at Cane Ridge. Outside the meeting house people were groaning and falling to the ground. Some fell and were unconscious, others were conscious. A few fell into a deep coma. Crowds gathered around each person who fell.[6] According to a minister named James Campbell, some "got through"—meaning coming to assurance of salvation; others never did. Those who succeeded often arose with shouts of joy and began their own exhortations. There were several people exhorting simultaneously in various parts of the grounds. According to Campbell:

> Sinners dropping down on every hand, shrieking, groaning, crying for mercy, convoluted; professors praying, agonizing, fainting, falling down in distress, for sinners, or in raptures of joy! Some singing, some shouting, clapping their hands, hugging and even kissing, laughing; others talking to the distressed, to one another, or to opposers of the work, and all this at once—no spectacle can excite a stronger sensation.[7]

The endless activity never quite ceased for the first two days, even in the early morning hours. Some people stayed up all night. Fatigued ministers were continually in demand to attend the slain, to pray with the penitent and to calm the hysterical.

Perhaps most impressive to many spectators were the exhortations. Here and there almost anyone, including those who rose from the ground as well as child converts, might burst out with an exhortation. Women, small children, slaves, shy people, and illiterate people all exhorted with great effect. Observers marveled at their eloquence, their deep feeling, and often their seeming preternatural understanding of Scripture.

Some believed the newly converted enjoyed the gift of prophecy, while critics often believed them possessed by demons. One observer who arrived at Cane Ridge on

Saturday when the revival was nearing its peak estimated that three hundred people exhorted, many at the same time.

It is reported that a seven-year-old girl mounted a man's shoulders and spoke wondrous words until she was completely fatigued. Then she lay her head on his as if to sleep. A person in the audience suggested that the poor thing had better be laid down, presumably to sleep. The girl aroused at this suggestion and said, "Don't call me poor, for Christ is my brother, God my father, and I have a kingdom to inherit, and therefore do not call me poor, for I am rich in the blood of the Lamb."[8]

The peak day was Sunday, when Presbyterians were presiding at Communion. Some Methodists, as I said above, felt excluded. The Presbyterians gave their scheduled sermons from the tent. A Methodist minister decided to move to a fallen tree a hundred feet east of the meetinghouse and made this his pulpit. His opening prayer and hymn gave him a huge audience—estimated between ten and fifteen thousand. He took his text from 2 Corinthians 5:10, "For we must all appear before the judgment seat of Christ, that each one may receive his recompense in the body, according to what he has done, whether it was good or bad." As he spoke hundreds fell. Between that Sunday and Wednesday it is reported that no fewer than five hundred people were on the ground.

By Monday, however, many visitors had to leave and return to their jobs. New arrivals kept coming until Wednesday or Thursday. Then all began to leave and return to their homes. The Cane Ridge Revival lasted about six days, with the greatest intensity on the Saturday and Sunday. The New England Awakening lasted for several years; America's "second great awakening" lasted only several days.

AFTER THE REVIVAL

The Cane Ridge Revival has been called America's Pentecost. The manifestations were unplanned. They emerged spontaneously when Christians met and began to worship. They happened during Communion. During preaching. But no doubt pigeon religion crept in too. Some probably faked the manifestations. Some fell off horses, sustaining minor cuts and bruises. I doubt that any true revival comes in a neat and tidy package.

One of the great evidences that Cane Ridge was a genuine outpouring of the Spirit was when so many who came to scoff and oppose were suddenly converted to Christ instead. The manifestations did not happen to any particular class, educated or uneducated. Many leading citizens were deeply affected, beginning with the governor of Kentucky. A representative to the Kentucky assembly was so affected by the revival that he gave up politics and became a minister. A number of Presbyterian ministers with degrees experienced convulsions or fell into comas. It should be said too that at least two-thirds of those who fell to the ground were women or girls. Said Conkin, "No aerobic exercise could match some of the jerking and dancing...Those affected, some at the cost of great embarrassment, invariably agreed that what they did was involuntary. They could not help it...Scarcely anyone present seemed immune to some physical effects."[9]

Estimates of those slain ranged from one thousand to three thousand. Estimates of conversions also ranged from one thousand to three thousand. A year later, a visitor to Lexington said that there was still talk everywhere about the revival in Cane Ridge.

It was supposedly a Presbyterian affair, but as Conkin put it, "the Methodists did it better."[10]

Peter Cartwright (1785–1872), who became a famous Methodist revivalist, gave this testimony:

> To this meeting [at Cane Ridge 1801] I repaired, a guilty, wretched sinner. On the Saturday evening of said meeting, I went, with weeping multitudes, and bowed before the stand, and earnestly prayed for mercy. In the midst of a solemn struggle of soul, an

impression was made on my mind, as though a voice said to me, "Thy sins are all forgiven thee." Divine light flashed all around me, unspeakable joy sprung up in my soul. I rose to my feet, opened my eyes, and it really seemed as if I was in heaven...and though I have been since then, in many instances, unfaithful, yet I have never, for one moment, doubted that the Lord did, then and there, forgive my sins.[11]

> *One of the great evidences that Cane Ridge was a genuine outpouring of the Spirit was when so many who came to scoff and oppose were suddenly converted to Christ instead.*

The Cane Ridge Revival ultimately caused a lot of division. At its peak—as on the Saturday and Sunday—theological divisions seemed as nothing. Barton Stone would say that it did not matter whether you were Baptist, Presbyterian, or Methodist; only that you were a Christian. But sadly he later founded what would be yet another denomination—the Christian Church. In the meantime he changed his theological views and became Arminian.

Presbyterians also split. A remnant became the Cumberland Presbyterian Church. They held to parts of the Westminster Confession of Faith—which emphasizes predestination—but welcomed Methodist theology too.

J. O. McClurkan, the founder of Trevecca College, was a Cumberland Presbyterian. He moved to Nashville. When G. Campbell Morgan, one of my predecessors at Westminster Chapel, was preaching in Nashville, he met J. O. McClurkan. McClurkan told Morgan that he wanted to start a school but did not know what to call it. Campbell Morgan suggested that McClurkan call his school Trevecca, named for the Trevecca College in Wales. Trevecca College in Wales was founded as a place where Arminians and Calvinists could work together. When Trevecca became a part of the Church of the Nazarene, it was named Trevecca Nazarene College (now University) which is, as some readers may recall, my own Alma Mater.

Barton Stone lamented that the Cane Ridge Revival did not go on and on, noting years later: "These blessed effects would have continued, had not men put forth their hallowed hands to hold up the tottering ark, mistaking it for the ark of God."[12] Pigeon religion moved in when people tried their best to pretend that the anointing of the Spirit was still on them. Some did this by faking it, some by unconsciously assuming that if they had the same "effects" it meant they had the anointing! Pigeon religion.

I close this chapter with my own observation about the various effects. When the Cane Ridge Revival was at its height and preachers exhorted on the grounds, they developed a recognizable *sound* in their voices which came from difficulty in getting their breath as they spoke. Those who were present in the Welsh Revival (1904–05) reported that they would at times feel a need to take a breath because of the *kabodh*—the weight of glory—on them. The same thing happened at Cane Ridge, preachers sometimes gasping for breath as they spoke.

I suspect it was very real and uncontrived during the height of the revival. However, it became easy to imitate after the revival waned. It lasted for many years. I used to hear some preachers in Ashland, Kentucky (one hundred miles from Cane Ridge) preach the same way. "For God-uh so loved the world-uh, that He gave His only begotten-uh Son-uh, and whosoever believes-uh would not perish-uh, but have everlasting life-uh." (That's the best way I know to spell it).

During the final week of writing this manuscript, I happen to be in North Carolina. I turned on a local channel and listened to a preacher. He was doing the same thing after two or three minutes into his sermon—ending "uh" after every three or four seconds.

I don't know if these preachers knew what they were doing. As I look back it is clear to me that they managed to produce the "effect"—which convinced some people that the old anointing was still around—without the true anointing of the Spirit. They called it "unction." In Wales a certain type of anointing was called the "hoyle."

Pigeon religion is, I fear, unavoidable in the end. As I keep saying, none of us is perfect. Even the greatest revivals and awakenings all come to an end. Like the Galatians, we begin in the Spirit but so often fancy ourselves to be perfected by the flesh—not realizing it is the flesh. As it is hard to tell the difference sometimes between a pigeon and a dove, so is it difficult to realize that pigeon religion can assert itself on what was once so real and precious.

Chapter 11

PROPHETIC RESPONSIBILITY

But above all things, my brothers, do not swear, either by heaven or by the earth or by any other oath. But let your "Yes" be "Yes" and your "No" be "No," that you do not fall into condemnation.

—JAMES 5:12

———— ◆ ————

**Pigeons love attention. Doves
do not love attention.**

————

I HAD NEVER HEARD of "prophetic ministry" until 1990. Until then prophecy—to me—meant stuff about the last days before the Second Coming. But when John Wimber brought the "Kansas City prophets" to London, my perception of the prophetic ministry took on an altogether different meaning. Sometime after these prophetic men made their impact on London, the book *Kansas City Prophets* appeared. The magazine *Christianity Today* featured the men in that book. As it happens, I got to know all four of the men fairly well, two of them very well.

I became close to John Paul Jackson, one of the so-called Kansas City prophets, who recently went to be with the Lord. I served on his board. His personal prophecies to me have been life changing. He always wanted to learn. I loved his position on the issue of "character more important than gifting," a highly needed emphasis nowadays. One evening over ten years ago, sitting at our dinner table in Key Largo, he looked at me suddenly and said, "RT, you will live to a ripe old age, but if you don't get in shape physically you won't be able to enjoy it." I was shaken, not only because I needed to do this but because his other prophetic words to me had been so amazingly accurate. I immediately changed my diet and lost weight. Steve Strang, my publisher, gave me an exercise program, which I have followed faithfully every morning for over ten years. I hired a trainer who has me lifting weights. I hate to think what my physical condition would be today had it not been for those words. At age eighty I travel the world and am in better shape than I was thirty years ago.

I was deeply influenced by another of these men. He became a member of Westminster Chapel. I can say he did us good, not harm. I learned a lot. It was a new world for me. I am certainly all the better for it, but I have also learned a lot that is not so good about the way prophetic ministry has developed in some fairly high-profile people.

The gist of most of this chapter was presented as a brief talk to some seventy of the better known prophetic people in America. Knowing exactly what I would say, John Paul asked me to address them at his Convergence Conference in the Dallas-Fort Worth area a couple years ago. I gave this address with some fear and trembling, knowing full well that I might be stepping on some of their toes—possibly every one of them. I must say, however, that *all* of them, so it seemed, agreed with me and thanked me for what I said.

"THE LORD TOLD ME"

Many people claim to speak for God these days, but how many of them really *do* speak for God? There are a lot of people who claim to have a prophetic gift and give out words introduced by "the Lord told me." The question is, how many of these words are truly from the Lord?

Should it bother us that so many words do not come to pass which were prefaced by the words "the Lord told me"?

And what do you suppose God in heaven thinks of all this?

Why is this chapter important? First, it is mainly because pigeon religion has swirled down vehemently on the prophetic ministry generally in America with a vengeance. Second, when a word does not come to pass which was introduced by "the Lord told me," obviously something has gone wrong. It dishonors the name of the Lord. It brings discredit upon the gift of prophecy generally, giving cessationists ammunition for their unbiblical hypothesis. Moreover, if the prophecy is not fulfilled after being told "the Lord told me," it is bearing false witness.

Should the people who claim that they have a word from the Lord apologize if it does not turn out as they promised? I hate to say it, but few do. Many do not have the humility to admit it when they got it wrong. When people are not gracious enough to admit when they got it wrong, it smacks of a lack of integrity. The matter could be largely resolved if such people would *stop* saying "the Lord told me" when making a pronouncement.

Why is it that people keep saying "the Lord told me" when they keep getting it wrong?

Nathan prophesied to David that he could build the temple, but had to come back the next day to admit he jumped the gun and that his word was not from God. He then told a disappointed David—who took it humbly—that Solomon, not David, would build the temple (2 Sam. 7). Samuel was convinced that Eliab would be the next king but climbed down before Jesse and all his sons and anointed David with oil (1 Sam. 16:6–12). We need more Nathans and Samuels today.

But does not God sometimes truly speak to us? Certainly. Then should we not attribute such a word to Him? Is there a right time for saying "the Lord told me" when one has a word they feel is *truly* from God? Is it not an encouragement when a prophetic person who has a solid reputation says, "the Lord told me to tell you this"? I will deal with these questions later in this chapter.

Prophecy—if it is a true prophecy—is a word directly from God unfiltered by human embellishment whether it refers to the past, present, or future.

Saying that "the Lord told me" is a habit that prophetic people find hard to break. Some feel it is almost impossible to break that habit. I pleaded with one of them to stop it. He tried. He couldn't. But he kept getting it wrong too.

I will come clean. Although I don't claim to have a prophetic gift, I have still made the same mistake thousands of times, whether it be to a person, "The Lord gave me a word for you," or when preaching, "The Lord gave me this sermon," "The Lord gave me this insight." When I do this I am claiming that God is behind all I say and that the people had better take it—or else. It must make the angels blush.

Prophecy—if it is a true prophecy—is a word directly from God unfiltered by human embellishment whether it refers to the past, present, or future. That said, there are levels of prophecy. Not all prophecy is of the same caliber or type.

SIX LEVELS OF PROPHECY

Picture a pyramid, starting at the bottom:

1. *General exhortation*, or encouragement, to an individual or congregation. This is the "lowest" level of prophecy. The possibility of prophesying like this is offered to *all* Christians. When Paul urged the Corinthian Christians to value the gift of prophecy more than speaking in tongues, he was not challenging them to be an Isaiah or Elijah. "But he who prophesies speaks to men for their edification and exhortation and comfort" (1 Cor. 14:3). God may indeed give a word of encouragement that should be shared with one or many.

2. *Specific warnings.* This is a higher level of prophecy. Agabus, referred to as a prophet by Luke, foretold that a severe famine would spread over the entire Roman world, which came to pass (Acts 11:27–28). The same Agabus warned Paul not to go to Jerusalem. Agabus took Paul's belt, tied his own hands and feet with it, and said, "The Holy Spirit says, 'In this manner the Jews at Jerusalem shall bind the man who owns this belt and deliver him into the hands of the Gentiles'" (Acts 21:11). Two things should be noted: first, Agabus said "The Holy Spirit says"—which is tantamount to saying, "The Lord told me." Second, when you examine what happened to Paul later in the Book of Acts, you will find that this is *not* what happened. The general warning that Paul would be in trouble with the Jews came to pass, yes; but Paul actually thwarted the Jews' plans—which in any case were certainly not handing him over to Gentiles. Moreover, Paul went to Rome because he himself demanded to be tried by Caesar (Acts 25:12). This meant that Agabus got one out of two prophecies right, but the one where he got the details totally wrong was when he said, "The Holy Spirit says." This is not exactly a good precedent for us to say, "The Lord told me." Sorry, but that is pigeon religion.

3. *When called before the authorities for the sake of Christ.* Jesus said, "You will be brought before governors and kings for My sake, for a testimony against them and the Gentiles. But when they deliver you up, take no thought of how or what you will speak. For it will be given you at that time what you will speak. For it is not you who speak, but the Spirit of your Father who speaks through you" (Matt. 10:18–20). This is yet a higher level of prophecy than the previous two levels.

As I mentioned earlier in this book, in 1963 when I was pastor of a church in Ohio, some of the members took exception to my theology. They reported me to the authorities of this denomination. I was asked to face a group of preachers that sat in judgment on what I had preached. On the morning of this public trial, my reading for the day was

Matthew 10:18–20, the passage quoted above. It gave me great comfort. On that evening when I faced both the "hierarchy" of this denomination and certain members of my church, I was not only given an amazing peace but a flow of words that I knew did not come from me.

I read this same passage to the late Yasser Arafat, letting him know I was claiming this scripture when I came to see him! He liked it because it compared him to a king! Although this passage did not truly fit—I was not visiting him owing to persecution—I still leaned on it, determining to take no thought in advance what I would say to him. I would not push what I am about to say too far, but I can truly state that I was always given words to say to Arafat that seemed appropriate at the time. I always emphasized that Jesus *died* on the cross, and prayed that the blood of Jesus would be sprinkled on Arafat by the Holy Spirit. He clearly loved it when I prayed like that. As I say in my book *It Ain't Over Till It's Over,* I would not be surprised to see Yasser Arafat in heaven.

These things said, we have a promise of genuine prophetic utterances should we be called to stand before authorities for what we believe.

4. *Preaching in the Spirit.* This is the way I would describe Peter's word that "If anyone speaks, let him speak as the oracles of God" (1 Pet. 4:11). This is surely a reference to preaching: an encouragement to those of us who are responsible for preaching the Word of God. We are actually encouraged to preach as if God were speaking through us. When I read these words I say, "If only!" I have been preaching for over sixty years. I think, just maybe, I have fulfilled 1 Peter 4:11 *twice.*

In any case, we as ministers are encouraged to believe that we *should* speak as though it were the Holy Spirit speaking through us. It would seem therefore that expository preaching should do that—that is, if our unfolding of Scripture is absolutely what God would dictate and not our private views. In a perfect world all preaching would be uttering the very oracles of God, but I fear we ministers all sadly come short of this.

5. *The noncanonical biblical prophets.* This level of prophecy would include prophets like Elijah, Elisha, Nathan, and Gad. "Non-canonical" means these prophets do not have a book with their name like Isaiah, Daniel, or Samuel. This is a very high level of prophetic utterances indeed. But even they were not perfect. Possibly the greatest anointing of the Spirit ever was on Elijah when he confronted the prophets of Baal on Mount Carmel: "How long will you stay between two opinions? If the LORD is God, follow Him, but if Baal, then follow him" (1 Kings 18:21). Elijah and the true God were openly vindicated before all those present when the fire of God fell before their very eyes (1 Kings 18:38). And yet in all this there was a frail, self-centered Elijah who made a claim that was utterly false: "I alone remain a prophet of the LORD" (1 Kings 18:22). Pigeon religion crept in even under such an extraordinary anointing. What Elijah said was patently false. Only days before, Elijah had run into Obadiah, who had hidden a hundred prophets in a cave to protect them from the wicked King Ahab (1 Kings 18:4–7). Elijah was not the only prophet left. He took himself too seriously.

The relevant question is, could there be noncanonical prophets like Elijah or Elisha today? I suspect there have been a few—very few—who have uttered words that are virtually as astonishing as some of those spoken by noncanonical prophets of the Old Testament. I could relate some of these, but I would prefer not to do it here, much less to mention names. In any case, though some of these men (some alive, some deceased) have uttered phenomenal words and have seen miracles as well, they are frail men of dust. This is partly why James said that Elijah was "a man subject to natural passions as we are" (James 5:17).

I believe that the greatest outpouring of the Holy Spirit is at hand. It is my view that the next thing to happen on God's calendar is not the Second Coming but rather what I call "the

Midnight Cry"—when the church is awakened before the Second Coming. God willing, this will be the subject of my next book. The Holy Spirit will come in the same power that we read about in the Book of Acts. It will be when the Word and the Spirit come together in a measure we have not seen to date. That is coming soon. Very soon. It would not surprise me if God raised up some Elijahs and Elishas when this happens. But even then such prophets will be under Holy Scripture; otherwise, how will we know they are true servants of God?

Question: But would a prophet speaking at this level not have the right to say, "The Lord told me" or, "Thus saith the Lord"? No. First, who is going to claim he or she has this "fifth level" of prophetic anointing? That would be pompous. But some will! One of my publishers told me that he had a writer who would not permit an editor to correct his material! He said that "God wrote this book." Therefore, the problem is, some will claim they have the authority of an Elijah or Elisha! They will make themselves exceptions to the principles I am suggesting in this chapter and claim the right to say, "Thus says the Lord." If one needs this prop to bolster his authority, he is not fit to prophesy. Elijah did not use the Mount Carmel platform to say, "The Lord told me to say this." If he had he would have brought the Lord down to his fleshly level when I said, "I alone am left."

It is my view that the next thing to happen on God's calendar is not the Second Coming but rather what I call "the Midnight Cry"—when the church is awakened before the Second Coming.

Prophets need to be humble. I might have called this chapter Prophetic Pride. Some of them love the limelight. They, like pigeons, want to be seen. They love attention. The dove—the true symbol of the Holy Spirit—does not seek or want attention.

6. *Holy Scripture.* This is the peak of the pyramid. This is supreme. The Bible is the highest level of prophecy. Moreover, this level is God's *final* revelation. There will never be a level of prophecy or an anointing of any prophet that will surpass or even equal the Bible. Like it or not, you and I must believe that. Otherwise the floodgates will be opened to every Tom, Dick, or Harry who falsely claims to be a mouthpiece of God. You can expect false prophets. How do we know the false from the true? The Bible. Dr. Martyn Lloyd-Jones frequently said, "The Bible was not given to replace the miraculous; it was given to correct abuses."

The Bible is God's ultimate and only infallible revelation. Any true prophet will *gladly* submit himself or herself to Holy Scripture. If they will not, reject them!

The entire Bible may justly be called prophecy. "But know this first of all, that no prophecy of the Scripture is a matter of one's own interpretation. For no prophecy at any time was produced by the will of man, but holy men moved by the Holy Spirit spoke from God" (2 Pet. 1:20–21). This refers to every word of the Old Testament. Paul said virtually the same thing: "All Scripture is inspired by God and is profitable for teaching, for reproof, for correction, and for instruction in righteousness" (2 Tim. 3:16). "All Scripture" means the Old Testament. What about the New Testament? The same thing is true. Peter affirmed Paul's writing as Scripture (2 Pet. 3:15–16). Paul equally claimed the same authority (1 Cor. 7:10; 14:37).

You and I will never outgrow the need for Scripture. The fastest way to become "yesterday's man or woman" is to fancy that we don't need to submit to Scripture. Remember, King Saul felt compelled to go against Scripture (1 Sam. 13:12). In that moment he became yesterday's man. The same will happen to you and me if we repeat Saul's folly.

The Bible is God's final, perfect, and infallible revelation of Truth. It will never be replaced or superseded before Jesus's second coming.

LIMITS OF PROPHECY

Every anointing has its limit. One of the most humbling things about the anointing is coming to terms with your limitations. Here is an extremely relevant passage:

> For I say, through the grace given to me, to everyone among you, not to think of himself more highly than he ought to think, but to think with sound judgment, according to the measure of faith God has distributed to every man. For just as we have many parts in one body, and not all parts have the same function, so we, being many, are one body in Christ, and all are parts of one another. We have diverse gifts according to the grace that is given to us: if prophecy, according to the proportion of faith.
> —ROMANS 12:3–6

When Paul says "if" a person's gift is prophecy, that is an important "if." I don't claim to have this gift—unless you take this passage as John Calvin did. He believed that Paul was talking about preaching. If that is what Paul means by the gift of prophecy, then I have the gift of prophecy. But I don't think that is what Paul means. I think Paul means what we have been writing in this chapter—prophecy that is a direct word from God. He could mean what I call Level One—the "lowest" level—or perhaps much higher than that. Regardless, Paul teaches that one must (1) discover what his or her anointing is, then (2) if it is prophesying, remember these words—"according to the proportion of faith."

There are two ways of interpreting proportion (Gr. *analogia*): extent or analogy. If Paul means the *extent* of faith—which he certainly does—one must prophesy *within* that limit of faith. As I've mentioned previously, we all have faith in measure. That means there is a limit to our faith. Only Jesus had the Holy Spirit without limit. Only Jesus had a perfect faith. Some people with a true gift of prophecy go *beyond* the limit they are given—and get into trouble. Sometimes a person will get a true word from God but will then embellish it. Pigeon religion. If we stay within the limit of our faith, we will be safe. "Do not go beyond what is written" (1 Cor. 4:6, NIV) is a word for prophets and preachers.

But if Paul means *analogy*—which he also certainly does— one must prophesy according to sound theology. The Greek in Romans 12:6 is literally to be translated that we prophesy according to the "analogy of faith." This means comparing Scripture with Scripture. This is why Calvin thought prophesying meant preaching. But if we accept that Paul meant *both* "extent" of faith—that is, a limit—and "analogy" of faith— that is, sound teaching—then we have the balanced picture. In a word: a prophet must stay within the limit of his faith but be sure he or she is sound in their teaching. If what he or she prophesies goes against New Testament teaching, the prophecy is to be rejected.

A true prophet will proclaim what is within the circle of orthodoxy—sound teaching. I'm sorry, but there are prophetic people at large who say weird things—"off the wall" teaching that is heretical and embarrassing. Fancy this: an angel tells a prophet that there is "no need to talk about Jesus—everybody has heard about Him. You should talk about angels." This is an extreme example, of course, but it does show how far away some prophetic people are from solid New Testament teaching. I am not saying that a prophet needs to be a learned theologian. But I am saying he should be sound in what he believes about God, man, sin, and salvation.

Paul said, "For we know in part, and we prophesy in part" (1 Cor. 13:9). Think about that for a moment. How humbling: we know in part. We don't know everything! Elisha did not know everything. True, he might tell a king what he says in his bedroom (2 Kings 6:12), but only if *God* deigns to reveal such to him. Elisha did not know everything. No prophet knows everything. No theologian knows everything. Paul did not know everything. Satan does not know everything. Only God knows everything. And He may choose to reveal *some* things to *some* people. But if He withholds information or revelation, there is nothing that anybody can do about it. God is sovereign. He shows mercy on whom He will (Rom. 9:15). God may choose not to speak to a whole generation. As the word of the Lord was once called "rare" (1 Sam. 3:1)—meaning there was no prophet who spoke for God at the time—so can there be "a famine...of hearing the words of the LORD" (Amos 8:11).

In a word: a prophet must stay within the limit of his faith but be sure he or she is sound in their teaching. If what he or she prophesies goes against New Testament teaching, the prophecy is to be rejected.

He may not speak on a particular occasion. One problem that prophetic people have nowadays is that they are invited to preach but are required to "produce the goods" and call out people to show they are lively prophets. To be very candid, it is my view in my old age that a sad turn for prophetic people was when they began to call out people publicly from the pulpit. People don't come to hear them preach; they come to hear a "word of knowledge" or prophetic word. I know exactly what I am talking about. Many sincere souls come hoping, hoping, hoping that their name will be called out and they will be given a definite word.

You will ask, "What is wrong with that?" I answer: It puffs the prophet's ego. He gets the attention. He loves it. Like pigeons.

It is my view that if a prophetic person has a word for someone, he or she should send for them. Why does he need to show his gift before hundreds or thousands?

If, however, a prophet has a word for the entire congregation, that is different. All need to hear it. But individuals for whom a word was given can be sent for. One problem is, some of these people want to preach. Good. Nothing wrong with that. If they have that gift, they should preach. But their words of knowledge or personal prophecies should be kept secret.

THE HONOR OF GOD

We come now to the real reason one should not use the phrase, "The Lord told me." It is owing to the spiritual inter-pretation of the Third Commandment:

> You shall not take the name of the LORD your God in vain, for the LORD will not hold guiltless anyone who takes His name in vain.
>
> —EXODUS 20:7

In the Sermon on the Mount, Jesus gave His interpreta-tion of the Mosaic Laws. He interpreted them *spiritually*. For example, the sixth commandment says: "You shall not murder" (Exod. 20:13). But Jesus said, "But I say to you that whoever is angry with his brother without a cause shall be in danger of the judgment" (Matt. 5:22). Whereas the Mosaic Law only required punishment for the person who physically murdered another, Jesus said that murder in the heart was sin in the sight of God. Later on Jesus applied this spiritual interpretation to refer to forgiving one's enemy and praying for them to be blessed (Matt. 5:44).

When Jesus referred to the seventh commandment, "You shall not commit adultery" (Exod. 20:14), He gave His own take on it: "But I say to you that whoever looks on a woman to lust after her has committed adultery with her already in his heart" (Matt. 5:28). The Mosaic Law only referred to physical adultery, but Jesus said that lusting is committing adultery in one's heart. This would condemn pornography, one of the greatest secret sins of many Christians today.

Jesus's interpretation of the third commandment—about

taking the name of the Lord in vain, or misusing it—came in Matthew 5:33–37, which deals with the issue of swearing an oath. The bottom line: do not use the name of the Lord when swearing an oath. In fact, Jesus said not to swear at all! This does not refer to using foul language, although that is certainly condemned by these verses. He is referring to using the name of the Lord when claiming to tell the truth. In ancient times it was proper to swear an oath. Indeed, the Old Testament required it. But when they swore an oath they swore by something or someone "greater," as Hebrews 6:13 puts it. In ancient times it was one thing to break a promise—which, of course, one shouldn't do. But if they broke an *oath*, it was reprehensible. So in order to convince another person they were telling the truth, they swore an oath and did so by the name of God Almighty or the name of another god or gods, such as when Jezebel said, "May the gods deal with me, be it ever so severely" (1 Kings 19:2, NIV). The point is, they said what they needed to say to make sure they were believed!

That said, there is such a thing as God Himself swearing an oath to us. The first time this happened in the Bible was when He swore an oath to Abraham—one of the greatest things that can happen to anybody. But because God could find no greater, He swore by Himself (Heb. 6:13). What the oath did for Abraham was this: he knew absolutely and totally that his seed would be "as numerous as the stars in the sky" (Gen. 22:17, NIV). In other words, when God swore an oath it was *as good as done*. Doubts were no more.

When Elijah told King Ahab that it would not rain "except by my word" (1 Kings 17:1), how could he be so sure? He calmly told the king: "No rain until I say so." That's a pretty bold thing to say! But Elijah was not worried. Why? God swore an oath to him that it would not rain. This actually came in answer to Elijah's prayer that it would not rain (James 5:17). And God assured Elijah with an oath that it would not rain. How do we know that? Because in 1 Kings 17:1 Elijah said to Ahab, *"As the* LORD *God of Israel lives* before whom I stand, there will not be dew or rain these years except by my word" (emphasis added).

That is oath language. Whenever you see that phrase it means an oath was sworn. In Elijah's case it was an oath that God swore to him. That was why he was so calm and sure when he confronted Elijah. That said, when Elijah brought in God's name—"As the Lord God of Israel lives"—he was implicitly telling Ahab how he knew that it would not rain: *God told him.* Simple as that. Therefore Elijah was saying, "The Lord told me." You might say, "Surely that proves that we can say that the Lord told us, since Elijah said it." Perhaps. But read on.

When you or I make the claim, "God told me," we are assuring those who hear us of one thing: *God has sworn an oath to me.* This therefore means that what I prophesy *will come to pass.* There is no fear, worry, anxiety, or doubt about it: if God swears to you or me, what we say will come to pass.

Question: What if God *really has sworn an oath to us? Should we not therefore say so?* Answer: no. This is because Elijah was living in the time of the Old Testament and the Mosaic Law, when one was commanded and encouraged to swear an oath. Jesus changed that. His interpretation of the third commandment led Him to say, "Do not swear at all."

But there is a further problem: how do you know when God has sworn an oath to you? I hope I will not be unfair to say that if you have to ask that question you have not experienced His oath. When God swears an *oath,* you are left without doubt. You won't need to ask the question, "Did God swear an oath to me?" To put it another way, there is no sign in northwest Arizona that says, "You are now looking at the Grand Canyon." No sign is needed. When you come to that breathtaking spot, you know it's the real thing.

Moreover, if God *has* sworn an oath to you that leads to you know a certain thing is going to happen, you don't need to tell how you know it! *Just say it.* You don't need to say to someone, "The Lord told me you should take this job."

Just say, "You should take this job." They will say, "How do you know?" You say, "Because you should." To throw in the name of the Lord will probably not convince them. Don't abuse His name in an effort to bolster your authority!

In November 1954 I was privileged to have conversations with Dr. John Sutherland Logan when I was a student at Trevecca. At breakfast one morning I asked, "Dr. Logan, how can I know whether I am called to preach? I am struggling with this. Will I ever know for sure?"

His reply: "You are."

I said, "How can I know?"

He said it again, "You are."

A third time I said, "I need to know for sure!"

"You are."

That is all he would say. And guess what—I believed him. I never looked back, neither did I ever doubt it. He never said, "The Lord told me." He simply spoke with a calm authority, and I knew I had heard from God.

But there is another issue here. It is the elephant in the room. What is the *real* reason I would say to you, "The Lord told me"? Is it to make *the Lord* look good? Or is it to give myself credibility with you? That is the real meaning of "misusing" God's name as in the third commandment. It is precisely why Jesus gave His spiritual interpretation of this command; it is why He said:

> But I say to you, do not swear at all: neither by heaven, for it is God's throne; nor by the earth, for it is His footstool; nor by Jerusalem, for it is the city of the great King. Nor shall you swear by your head, because you cannot make one hair white or black. But let your "Yes" mean "Yes," and "No" mean "No." For whatever is more than these comes from the evil one.
>
> —MATTHEW 5:34–37

You may not have realized you were swearing, or breaking Jesus's word, when you said, "The Lord told me." I do not want to make anybody feel guilty. We have all done this, just as we have all lusted and hated in our hearts. But if we want to raise the credibility of the prophetic, this is one thing we can do: stop using the Lord's name to enhance our credibility. Our aim should be to make *God* look good, not to make ourselves look good.

But should we not honor God by giving Him the *credit* if we are convinced that He has given us a word? This is a dilemma I sympathize with. But I would say that the Lord knows you are thankful and want to honor Him. You can thank Him yourself. It would surely be OK to say, "I think the Lord has given me a word for you," or, "I feel I have a word from the Lord for you." There is nothing wrong with that. You have shown a bit of humility by not making an outright claim that He is your authority.

At the end of the day the person you wish to encourage will know whether it was the Lord who gave you the word. Your saying, "Thus saith the Lord," won't convince them—especially if it does not come to pass. But if it comes to pass without your bringing the name of the Lord in, they will see for themselves it was from God. For that reason, it seems to me that it is better for *them* to conclude, "That was a word from the Lord." Best of all, you have not brought His name into your prophetic word.

> *But if we want to raise the credibility of the prophetic, this is one thing we can do: stop using the Lord's name to enhance our credibility. Our aim should be to make God look good, not to make ourselves look good.*

Ask yourself: Am I wanting to make the Lord look good or me look good?

Years ago I preached a sermon on James 5:12—which is at the beginning of this chapter—entitled "Name Dropping." We all have failed in this area, namely, wanting someone to know that we know a particular person. If I told you I know Billy Graham, would I be making him look good or me? I think you know the answer to that! But the worst kind of name-dropping is dropping the name of the Lord. That is what Jesus was speaking against. He is virtually saying, "Leave the name of the Lord out when it comes to making a statement to someone." God does not want that kind of credit!

I asked Bruce Atkinson, the associate pastor of London's Kensington Temple, whether he ever says, "Thus saith the Lord," when he wants to convince someone of something. His humorous reply: "Yes, when I'm losing an argument, when they won't do what I tell them, when I don't get my own way!" He was joking of course, but this unveils a lot of truth. It is so easy to use the Lord's name when we want to have control. We often use the Lord's name when we are struggling to be heard. It is an attempt to gain significance. It is pigeon religion.

Chapter 12

SEXUAL PURITY

For this is the will of God, your sanctification: that you should abstain
from sexual immorality, that each one of you should know how to possess
his own vessel in sanctification and honor, not in the lust of depravity, even
as the Gentiles who do not know God… the Lord is the avenger in all
these things… For God has not called us to uncleanness, but to holiness.

—1 THESSALONIANS 4:3–7

Pigeons will have more than one
mate. Doves have one mate for life.

NOTHING BRINGS DISGRACE upon the name of Christ
and the reputation of His church like sexual scandal.
Journalists love it. Non-Christians love it. The world
loves it. When Christians fall into sexual sin, it gives the
world an opportunity to say, "See there, they are no different
from us. Why should we believe they have something to offer
that we need?"

Many people avoid sexual affairs mainly for one reason:
they are afraid they will get caught. The wonderful thing
about Joseph, son of Jacob, who had the chance of a "safe"
affair, was this: he refused the flirtations of Potiphar's wife
for two reasons: (1) he knew that Potiphar totally trusted
him, and (2) God would know. "How then can I do this great
wickedness and sin against God?" (Gen. 39:9).

When I say it was a "safe" affair, I mean there was minimal likelihood they would get found out. First, Mrs. Potiphar wasn't going to tell her husband, an Egyptian officer. Joseph was a Hebrew slave. She would not lower herself to admit she had an affair with a person of that class. Second, nobody back in Canaan would ever find out; Joseph's father and brothers were a long way from Egypt.

But Joseph refused her. He could not have known that he had been earmarked to be prime minister of Egypt down the road. It was part of his testing and preparation.

"It seems that the devil gets 75 percent of God's best servants through sexual temptation," said Billy Graham. The irony is that even his own family has recently experienced this. It is so sad. Hardly a day goes by nowadays that one of the high-profile servants of God is not caught in an affair. And yet—to be utterly candid with you—when I hear of a minister who falls into sexual sin I have to say, "That could be me. I am without excuse if I pour scorn on such a person and judge them. For there go I but by the sheer grace of God."

Not only that; Jesus was more compassionate in the area of sexual sin than any other. He was ruthless when it came to the self-righteous Pharisees. But when a woman was found having committed adultery, Jesus did two things. First, He said, "Let him who is without sin among you be the first to throw a stone at her" (John 8:7). By that Jesus was showing that we all are weak by nature in that area. Second, He asked her where her accusers were. She said there were none. Jesus then added, "Neither do I condemn you. Go and sin no more" (v. 11).

Along the way anyone who has been earmarked for a lofty position is being tested and prepared to see if they can be trusted with greatness.

That Jesus would say, "Neither do I condemn you," is interpreted by some to mean that sexual sin is to be excused and overlooked, that God hated self-righteousness so much more, so let's not be so hard on sexual sin. Wrong. I reply: Yes, sexual desire is physical; God made us that way. This desire also comes from the need to be affirmed by the opposite sex; some feel it is a way of building up their self-esteem that they should attract the opposite sex to give in to temptation. Jesus concluded the matter by saying to this woman, "Go and sin no more." In other words, stop it. Furthermore, like it or not, God also set down laws in the Garden of Eden that indicated sex was to be enjoyed only by heterosexual monogamous and permanent marriage (Gen. 2:18, 23–25). Moreover, when Joseph said to Potiphar's wife, "How can I do this thing and sin against God?" it was *before* the Law of Moses had come along. The seventh commandment, "You shall not commit adultery" (Exod. 20:14), was affirming what had been true already.

Reader, what if you have been earmarked for a great inheritance down the road? What if you could be a future governor, senator, or president? What if you could be the next Billy Graham? What if you could be trusted one day with great wealth? Along the way anyone who has been earmarked for a lofty position is being tested and prepared to see if they can be trusted with greatness.

If you are in an affair as you read these lines—or are thinking about it—I have a word for you: STOP IT. Stop it *now*. It is only a matter of time before you would give a thousand worlds to roll the clock back to this moment. For all I know, God has led you to read this chapter in the nick of time to spare you incalculable agony and guilt.

GOD DOES NOT TEMPT US

I was surprised when Pete Cantrell, one of the greatest observers of pigeons and doves around in our day, said to me that pigeons will have more than one mate; a dove will have only one mate for life. This is another clear example of how the dove is a symbol of the Holy Spirit. The Holy Spirit will never, ever lead you to sin. God does not tempt us (James 1:13). He may allow a situation to develop in which temptation emerges—oh yes. But everyone is tempted when they are drawn away of their own lust and enticed. Never accuse God. That won't work.

Never before has there been such a need for Christian leaders to emphasize sexual purity in their teaching and exemplify it by their lives. What an embarrassment it is for faithful Roman Catholics to discover that so many of their leaders entered into the priesthood not out of love for God but for an opportunity to exploit their sexual desires. It is true of Protestant leaders as well; some take advantage of women coming to them for solid Christian counsel, only to be led into sexual promiscuity.

This is to say nothing of the ever-increasing high profile leaders in churches and on television who get caught being unfaithful to their wives. And one wonders how many carry on who don't get caught. Just remember this: "We must all appear before the judgment seat of Christ, that each one may receive his recompense *in the body*, according to what he has done, whether it was good or bad" (2 Cor. 5:10, emphasis added). The "good" here indicates a reward to those who disciplined themselves—whether heterosexual or homosexual—while in their earthly bodies. The "bad" indicates a clear judgment to those who chose to give in to temptation—whether heterosexual or homosexual—while in their earthly bodies.

Make no mistake: God has commanded our sanctification that we abstain from sexual sin (1 Thess. 4:3–7). Not only that; God "is the avenger in all these things, as we also have forewarned you," said Paul (v. 6). This shows that Paul preached against sexual sin. Preachers need to preach against sexual impurity and not sweep such issues under the carpet. People need to be *taught*. And *warned*. Sooner or later all will be in the open. "For nothing is secret that will not be revealed, nor anything hidden that will not be known and revealed," said Jesus Christ (Luke 8:17). Those who have not been granted repentance after falling into sin will be exposed before all. It is only a matter of time. "He will bring to light the hidden things of darkness" (1 Cor. 4:5).

I would like to think that God will use this chapter not only to awaken those who need this word but to put people on the right path before it is too late.

HYPER-GRACE TEACHING

In my book *Holy Fire* I warned of this modern teaching on grace that some call "hyper-grace." It seems to have come out of Singapore and Hong Kong, although I must say it is an ancient point of view. Some in Corinth held to what we now call hyper-grace. Paul wrote in 1 Corinthians 5:1, "It is actually reported that there is sexual immorality among you, and such immorality as is not even named among the Gentiles, that a man has his father's wife." This apparently meant that someone was sleeping with his stepmother.

"But you are arrogant," Paul went on in verse 2. This arrogance is the testimony of hyper-grace teaching, which says, "Do not worry if you fall into sin; it has been dealt with by Jesus's death on the cross. Don't worry about confessing sins; this is absolutely unnecessary; they have been dealt with at the cross!"

Says Paul: "Instead you should have mourned, so that he who has done this deed might be removed from among you" (v. 2). This is inescapable proof that if the Apostle Paul were around today, he would abominate hyper-grace teaching. And yet these people have the audacity to allege that Paul is the author of this teaching. Never! He would be scathing in his rebuke. He would disown those who claim to be following him.

When I first heard of this teaching a few years ago, I

predicted that it was only a matter of time before the grossest immorality would break out in the churches where this was taught. I still believe this. There will be wife swapping, homosexual promiscuity, and shameless carryings on under the name of grace. It is the inevitable outcome of a perversion of Paul's teaching of grace and holiness.

> *We are not saved by holy living; holiness is our way of saying thank you to God for saving us.*

A year ago I was disquieted to hear that the pastor of a very prominent church in Fort Lauderdale had begun preaching hyper-grace. What hurt me most was that I was a close friend of the founding pastor (now in heaven) and have preached there a number of times. I was shocked to hear of the things the new pastor was upholding. And then only a few weeks ago as I was writing this book—surprise, surprise—it was revealed that the new pastor has had an affair. His wife has had an affair. He is now out of the ministry—in shame and disgrace.

This is only the beginning. This teaching will result in widespread licentiousness. I pray that soon Christians will come to their senses and renounce this awful teaching. God has called us to holiness (1 Thess. 4:7; Heb. 12:14). We are not saved by holy living; holiness is our way of saying thank you to God for saving us.

Hyper-grace people would say "right on" with what I am saying now. But what they neglect to see is that every Christian is called to enter into his or her inheritance. Some do, some don't. Those who do will have a reward at the judgment seat of Christ. Those who don't will be shamefully exposed and dealt with at the judgment seat of Christ. Paul calls it being saved by fire (1 Cor. 3:15).

Hyper-grace people would drastically change the canon of Scripture; that is, they would eliminate certain books of the

New Testament (although some verses in those books they do accept). They especially stumble over Hebrews and 1 John. Those books so clearly contradict hyper-grace teaching. I have a word to any reader who has imbibed this teaching or is tempted to embrace it; it is the same warning I gave above to those in an affair or thinking about it: STOP IT. Now. It is only a matter of time before you would regret bitterly you gave such heresy the time of day.

PORNOGRAPHY

It would seem that some people live double lives and don't get caught. It is the mercy of God that some are not exposed— not for the sake of those involved but for the name and reputation of the church. I suppose that if every person in the church today involved in sexual impurity were suddenly found out, the walls of the church would fall, the foundations would crumble, and many churches would have to close their doors. For sexual impurity also includes pornography.

In the Old Testament a person could be involved in pornography without any guilt, for the Mosaic Law covered overt adultery. But Jesus's standard was much higher than that of the Law. Jesus said that lusting—or causing one to lust—is committing adultery in one's heart (Matt. 5:28). This categorically rules out pornography. And yet it is the chief sin of many ministers today. They can watch pornography in the privacy of their studies and nobody knows. But God knows. And the consequence is not only the forfeiting of the anointing of the Spirit but the forfeiting of a solid marriage.

Sexual purity therefore involves not only the body but the mind. Not only faithfulness in marriage but being faithful to one's spouse emotionally. Pigeons have more than one mate. Doves have one mate for life. The moment one gives in to lust for a woman not his wife, it is pigeon religion taking over.

For some this will be the most important chapter in my book. I pray it will do some good.

Chapter 13

"GIVE ME THAT OLD-TIME RELIGION"

Do not say, "Why were the earlier days better than these
days?" For it is not from wisdom that you inquire this.
—ECCLESIASTES 7:10

———— ✦ ————

**Pigeons have a homing instinct; they will return
to a cage. Doves will only return for survival.**

————

A FEW YEARS AGO I was being driven to the Cincinnati/Northern Kentucky International Airport. On the way I saw at a distance the old Union Terminal. It was once known as the most beautiful train station in the world and had more trains coming in and out of it than almost any in America. I said to the driver, "Do we have time to stop at the old Union Terminal?"

He said, "Yes, but why ever would you want to do this? It is now a shopping center."

I insisted that he take me to the station. He waited in the car as my mind went into nostalgic ecstasy. As a boy I went through that station hundreds of times with my parents. Nearly all passengers going any distance had to change trains in the Cincinnati station. We often had one or two hours between changes. It was then I would walk all over the station—a huge one—from one end to the other.

And now it was as if I were back "home." I took no notice of racks of clothes being sold or the rooms being occupied by clerks behind counters. There it was—the place where I spent hundreds of hours with my parents. I found myself uttering groans of blissful panting—"Oh. Oh. Mmm. Oh." It was like being elevated to the heavenlies. There was the old game room. There was the place where we ordered drinks. I found myself transported back over fifty years. It was like a glorious spiritual experience. Going back home.

I felt ashamed that I let myself get so carried away. I knew there was nothing spiritual about it at all. It was sheer nostalgia. But I still enjoyed it. When I got back to the car, I just wanted a time of quiet. It was pigeon religion. A pigeon has the homing instinct. Except he can actually go back to his cage.

I cannot do that. A few years ago I wanted our two children to see my old home on Hilton Avenue in Ashland, Kentucky. But the house bore no resemblance whatever to my childhood home. They had modernized it, cut down the old cherry tree, and removed the little fence that had separated our front yard from the back yard. I asked the present owners if they would allow me to have a look inside. They kindly obliged. But it was nothing like it used to be. It turned out to be a sad experience.

WE CANNOT GO HOME

But we try. And if there is an aroma, a sound, or a sight that takes us way back to childhood memories, we often feel so good and comfortable. I would pay a lot of money to taste my Grandma Kendall's green beans again. Or eat that pizza that you could get on Sunrise Boulevard in Fort Lauderdale many years ago. Or taste that Indian food around the corner from the Ealing Broadway tube station in west London. But those days are gone forever.

Home. Comfort zone. Where we feel safe. Unthreatened.

Nostalgia is a sentimental longing for the past, especially

when it is connected to happy associations. But could my desire to hear "Turn Your Eyes Upon Jesus" be my own nostalgic comfort zone? Certainly.

There is nothing wrong with being nostalgic or pining for a good feeling connected to happy associations with the past. Not only that, but also God can use these associations to lift us up. For instance, I find classical music to be very uplifting, both at church and at home.

My point is this. We should learn to know *why* we are having a "good feeling." It could be the presence of God. It could also be something that taps into our provincial yearning for what is familiar. We used to sing back in Ashland a song that dates back to 1873:

> Give me that old-time religion,
> Give me that old-time religion,
> Give me that old-time religion,
> It's good enough for me.[1]

I vividly recall some of the people in my old church jumping up and down in the aisles as they would burst into this song spontaneously. It had other repetitive verses, such as, "It was good for Paul and Silas" and "Makes me love everybody." This song became standard in many Protestant hymnals, although it says nothing about Jesus or the gospel. "Old-time religion" was a phrase that struck a chord, tapping into a rebellion against the more formal and liturgical type of worship.

I will never forget an occasion of a chapel service at Trevecca back in 1956. Having sung Isaac Watts's immortal hymn "When I Survey the Wondrous Cross," a student actually stood up and said, "Why are we singing these dead hymns? We need to be singing songs that have some life. We need revival." Those were his very words. He certainly did not reflect the views of the faculty or, perhaps, many of the students. But it was a dead giveaway he had no concept of the gospel of Christ, or he could not have spoken that way.

But songs in those days that had a faster beat and happy rhythm seemed to go along with a "revival spirit" and the need to avoid anything that was slow and quieter. To some the faster songs were a safeguard against formal worship which was thought to be worldly. The "livelier" songs became the norm and one's comfort zone for some reason.

Even the previously mentioned style of preaching that came out of the Cane Ridge Revival set the tone for a certain kind of speaking and exhortation. Preaching as if one was out of breath came to be called a "holy tone" and, if heard and recognized by some, gave people a feeling that the anointing was still around. Sadly, this became the standard for some. For example, in my old church, a person whose style was quiet and laid back was often perceived as unspiritual. Often, the louder the preacher, the more accepted he was. To them it was "old-time religion." The absence of the gospel or any mention of Jesus dying on the cross would not be noticed at all. I'm sorry, but that's the truth.

And yet the more liturgical churches have their nostalgic preferences too. People like this often prefer reading prayers to spontaneous praying. They feel safe this way. It is what makes people like this feel at home. Churches like the Free Church of Scotland will only sing psalms in church. People with that kind of background will be uncomfortable in a church that sings the hymns of Isaac Watts or John Newton. Should a psalm be brought into the order of service, people with this kind of background get a warm feeling—"Ah, that's better." For them it is home.

What then is "Holy Spirit religion"? How would an authentic anointing be recognized? How would we know that the Dove and not the pigeon has come down on the preacher? It is not always so clear—at least at first.

On the day following an address I gave at the Wembley Conference Centre in London in October 1992, I received a phone call from a London church leader. I had stressed the need for the Word and Spirit to come together and even forecast that the day was coming when we would see precisely this. I refer to this in the final chapter of my book *Holy Fire*.

This leader had one question: by "Word" did I mean "Reformed" theology? I knew exactly what he meant. He wanted to know if I would allow for the "Word "to include a teaching not totally reformed. Reformed teaching embraces the totally inability of man, election by God's sovereign will, and the eternal security of the true believer.

It was a fair question, a good question. I have thought long and hard about this. My answer is, not necessarily. For example, John Wesley was an extraordinary man of God. He was also the first major figure to popularize Arminianism—the belief that embraces the free will of man, election by foreseen faith, and the possibility that a saved person could be lost. I disagree with those tenets.

But God used John and Charles Wesley. Furthermore, where would the church be today without Charles Wesley's hymns? I thank God for the Wesley brothers.

Dr. Martyn Lloyd-Jones often quoted John Wesley and especially his view of the Holy Spirit. Dr. Lloyd-Jones always called himself a "Calvinistic Methodist." Whereas he rejected Arminianism, he embraced Wesley's belief in the immediate and direct witness of the Holy Spirit. Moreover, if Martyn Lloyd-Jones could accept Wesley, so can I. God used not only John and Charles Wesley but countless Arminian evangelists and leaders ever since. One should never forget that the central purpose of Wesleyanism is salvation.

SIX WAYS TO RECOGNIZE THE DOVE

What then would true religion look like? How would one recognize pigeon religion vis-à-vis dove religion? Here are the six cardinal issues for which we must be prepared to go to the stake:

> *Pigeon religion is the emphasis upon the
> things of the Holy Spirit without the gospel.
> When the message is only signs and wonders,
> words of knowledge, miracles, and the
> supernatural, God is not truly honored.*

1. The need to be saved or one will be eternally lost. This is the main thing. As the old cliché goes: the main thing is to keep the main thing the main thing. The Bible in a nutshell is this: "For God so loved the world that He gave His only begotten Son, that whoever believes in Him *should not perish* [be eternally lost], but have eternal life" (John 3:16, emphasis added).

At the end of the day, the most important article of faith in Christian theology is the need for all people to be saved. Once this belief is deleted, Christianity is no longer Christianity. For this reason our preaching must consistently proclaim the gospel. A ministry that does not keep this central has allowed pigeon religion to creep in. My criticism of the so-called Lakeland Revival of a few years back—and the reason I rejected it—came to this: I never heard the evangelist preach the gospel over those weeks. Not even once. It was pigeon religion.

Pigeon religion is the emphasis upon the things of the Holy Spirit without the gospel. When the message is only signs and wonders, words of knowledge, miracles, and the supernatural, God is not truly honored.

Pigeon religion is also an emphasis on the gospel without the Holy Spirit. However "sound" one's theology is, when a cessationist theology controls one's thinking, God is not honored as He *would* be were we fully open to His Spirit.

"Old-time religion" is a silly, sentimental, and worthless phrase unless it refers to the gospel of Jesus Christ that goes back to Golgotha and Pentecost.

2. *The way to be saved.* This too is the main thing: Jesus Christ and His death on the cross. "There is no other name under heaven given among men by which we must be saved" (Acts 4:12). Salvation is found in no other. There are three things to be clear about here: first, who Jesus *is*. He is the God-man. Jesus was and is God *as though* He were not man, and was and is man *as though* He were not God. "In the beginning was the Word, and the Word was with God, and the Word was God…the Word became flesh and dwelt among us" (John 1:1, 14).

Second, what Jesus *did*. He fulfilled the Law (Matt. 5:17), doing everything by His sinless life that is required for us to do, and died in our place. His shed blood turned the Father's wrath away. This is the heart of the gospel. "The Lord has laid on him the iniquity of us all" (Isa. 53:6). God punished Jesus for what we did; He was punished for our sins. Third, faith. All that Jesus did and suffered for the salvation of the human race is of no value *unless we believe*. Jesus died for all, yes. But until we believe, His death is of no worth to us. Our faith must be joined by His life and death or we will not be saved.

3. *The need for the Holy Spirit to bring us to Christ in faith.* Jesus said, "No one *can* come to Me unless the Father who has sent Me draws him" (John 6:44, emphasis added). When Jesus said no one "can" come to Him except by the Father, He was referring to two things. First, the utter inability of a person to move toward God unless enabled to do so. This is because we were born "dead" in trespasses and sins (Eph. 2:1). A dead man cannot do anything; he cannot speak or hear. You can shout to him, but he hears nothing. All of us are born like this, and we are not *able* to come to God in our own strength. Second, the need for the Holy Spirit to draw people to the Lord. When Jesus said no man is able come to Him unless he be drawn by the Father, He was referring to the Holy Spirit. "It is the Spirit who gives life. The flesh profits nothing" (John 6:63).

Why is this particular teaching important? It will stop us

from twisting people's arms to come to Christ. You can get them to the altar, but you cannot get them to Christ. You can lead a horse to the water, but you can't make him drink. Pigeon religion will get thousands to walk forward; only Dove religion will bring people to the foot of the cross.

4. *Being filled with the Holy Spirit.* "Be filled with the Spirit" (Eph. 5:18). If all Christians are already filled with the Holy Spirit merely because they are saved, Paul's words about being filled with the Spirit make no sense. All Christians have the Holy Spirit, yes (Rom. 8:9); one cannot come to the Lord Jesus apart from the Spirit (John 6:44).

But there is more. Call it what you will—baptism with the Spirit, sealing of the Spirit, or being filled with the Spirit—we all need *more* than what comes with conversion. Hence the question Paul put to the Ephesians: "Have you received the Holy Spirit since you believed?" (Acts 19:2). The answer: no. "Receiving the Spirit" was a phrase Paul used to denote a conscious experience. They knew they had not received the Spirit. When Paul asked the Galatians, "Did you receive the Spirit through the works of the law, or by hearing with faith?" (Gal. 3:2), he knew that they consciously received the Spirit after their conversion. As Dr. Martyn Lloyd-Jones put it, how could they know whether or not they received the Spirit unless it was a conscious experience?

Why would some people object to receiving the Holy Spirit after they have been converted? What are they fearful of? What are they nervous about? One would have thought saved people would *want* all they can get of God! But pigeon religion always opts for the comfort zone—what makes a person feel "good."

It is the devil, not the Holy Spirit, that would make a person feel threatened by the thought of "more." Moreover, if there is "more" than what I now have, I want it! Are you afraid you might have too much of God?

5. *The pursuit of holiness.* The way to walk in holiness is by living by the same Holy Spirit that enabled us to believe the

gospel. But what happens after we have believed? "This is the will of God, your sanctification" (1 Thess. 4:3). "As obedient children do not conduct yourselves according to the former lusts in your ignorance. But as He who has called you is holy, so be holy in all your conduct, because it is written, 'Be holy, for I am holy'" (1 Pet. 1:14–16).

As I mentioned earlier, every believer is called to come into his or her inheritance. Some do, some don't. Those who do will receive a "rich welcome" into the eternal kingdom (2 Pet. 1:11, NIV). They will receive a reward at the judgment seat of Christ (1 Cor. 3:14; 2 Cor. 5:10). Those who don't come into their inheritance will "suffer loss" of reward (1 Cor. 3:15).

The pursuit of holiness includes sexual purity, walking in total forgiveness, and refusing to settle for anything less than a closer walk with God.

I fear that some do not realize how serious God is when it comes to His people living holy lives. Those who give in to sexual sin, for example, incur His wrath (1 Thess. 4:6). The way to live a holy life is to walk in the Spirit. Those who do "shall not fulfill the lust of the flesh" (Gal. 5:16). Never forget that you are not your own. "You were bought with a price. Therefore glorify God in your body and in your spirit, which are God's" (1 Cor. 6:19–20).

6. *The infallibility of the Bible.* All Scripture is inspired by God (2 Tim. 3:16). Holy men of old wrote as they were borne along by the Holy Spirit (2 Pet. 1:20–21). This means that the Bible is infallible and reliable. Would you die for your faith in the infallibility of the Word of God? I would.

One could make a case for putting this sixth principle at the beginning. But we only know that the Bible is the Word of God by the internal testimony of the Holy Spirit. Therefore I put the need to be saved at the beginning. One is not required to believe in the infallibility of Scripture to become a Christian; it is what one comes to see afterward—by the Holy Spirit. This comes in time as a person walks with the Lord. I have been a Christian for seventy-four years. At the age of eighty, I believe in the infallibility and reliability of the Bible more than ever.

There is of course more to the Christian faith than these six principles. But these are what I believe most strongly. I would go to the stake for these. I would not go to the stake for my ecclesiology (doctrine of the church) or eschatology (doctrine of last things). Some sincere believers would bring even these into "old-time religion." I have outlined what I believe are the essentials of the faith for which I am willing to die. Call it what you will—"old-time," "old-fashioned," or whatever. Let's be sure that what we believe is what we would die for. And if it is good enough to die for, it is good enough to live for.

Chapter 14

COMMON GRACE

Every good gift and every perfect gift is from above and comes down from the Father of lights, with whom is no change or shadow of turning.

—JAMES 1:17

———◆———

**Pigeons get dependent on man for
food. Doves find their own food.**

———

Recently I complimented a cashier at our local supermarket. "You are always so pleasant and cheerful," I said to her. She is a middle-aged, dignified, pleasant woman. We have been shopping there for years, and I have always noticed how she stood out above the other people in the checkout lanes. So I spontaneously gave her the compliment.

Tears filled her eyes. "You have no idea how wonderful that makes me feel," she said.

I then asked her, "Where do you go to church?" fully expecting her to name a church in Hendersonville, Tennessee, a town right in the middle of the Bible Belt. She seemed to me to be a radiant Christian! The lady replied that she did not go to church at all, that she never had gone to church.

Whereas the lady was not the slightest bit offended, I was rather stunned that I had gotten it so wrong. I would have told you that she radiated Christ by her countenance.

Does this kind of story surprise you? I should not have

been surprised, but I was. My theology allows for a non-Christian to look like a genuine Christian. But when I got a sudden example of it, I was taken back. I thought *this* lady was a lovely Christian for sure! And what I don't enjoy talking about is how many *true* Christians at cash registers in stores can be so uncheerful and even rude!

My friend and colleague Charles Carrin made a similar observation about someone some time ago. When we checked into our hotel in Georgia, he spontaneously said to the receptionist, "Your face just shows the love of Jesus." I agreed. But we were wrong. She was a Hindu!

Generally speaking, there are basically two kinds of grace that flow from the throne of God: common grace and sovereign grace. Sovereign grace is God's special, saving grace. "For by grace you have been saved through faith, and this is not of yourselves. It is the gift of God, not of works, so that no one should boast" (Eph. 2:8–9). Common grace, however, is God's goodness to *all* humankind. It is a creation blessing and is not connected to salvation. God is the Creator of all men and women, whereas salvation is a gift only to those who believe. We call it "common" grace not because it is ordinary but because it is given commonly to every person, whether or not they are saved.

Common grace is therefore a creation gift, not a salvation gift. It is the explanation for your IQ, your talent, your love for science, music, art, or literature. It is the reason we have doctors, medicine, firemen, hospitals, and policemen. It is what keeps the world from being topsy-turvy, from being turned completely upside down. When you consider the depravity of all people by nature—the proneness to sin from our mother's womb—it is amazing that the world is no worse than it is! Common grace has nothing to do with salvation and everything to do with the fact that God is the Creator of all humankind. John Calvin called it "special grace in nature." That means that God is *kind to everyone*; He causes the sun to shine and the rain to fall on the just and the unjust (Matt. 5:45). Every good and perfect gift is from "above" (James 1:17).

Have you wondered why few Christians receive Nobel Prizes? Have you wondered why the greatest scientists, musicians, composers, engineers, architects, and kings are not Christians? This should not surprise us. And yet for reasons I don't fully understand, God's grace largely bypasses the rich, the nobility, the famous, and the high-powered people of this world.

> For observe your calling, brothers. Among you, not many wise men according to the flesh, not many mighty men, and not many noble men were called. But God has chosen the foolish things of the world to confound the wise. God has chosen the weak things of the world to confound the things which are mighty. And God has chosen the base things of the world and things which are despised. Yes, and He chose things which did not exist to bring to nothing things that do, so that no flesh should boast in His presence.
>
> —1 CORINTHIANS 1:26–29

The Countess of Huntingdon, a benefactor of George Whitefield, said that she was saved by the letter "m." Paul did not say not "any," but not "many" of noble birth are called! Therefore, once in a while God will convert an Augustine, an Athanasius, an Anselm, a Thomas Aquinas, a Martin Luther, a John Calvin, or a Jonathan Edwards. And when a high level of common grace coincides with saving grace, the whole world is changed! But those kinds of situations are few. We could wish for more, and we can certainly pray that God will save unusually gifted people. In the meantime we must get used to each other and accept that most people that are fellow Christians are ordinary, unspectacular folk.

And yet we must not limit common grace to unusual people. We *all* are the beneficiaries of common grace. We all have the same Creator. He has made us like we are. He chose the time and place of our birth (Acts 17:26). He chose our parents. He was looking after us long before we were converted. Peer pressures as we grew up, the friends at school, and our teachers and authority figures that shaped us are a part of God's common grace. Once we came to Christ in faith, we were given the Holy Spirit. We may therefore conclude that *God made us like we are.* He takes our past, our talents, our weaknesses, and strengths *plus* the Holy Spirit.

The difference between the Christian and the non-Christian is this: we have the Holy Spirit; they don't. They have their gifts and talents and learning *without* the Holy Spirit. We have our gifts and talents and learning *plus* the Holy Spirit.

But our level of common grace may not be as high as the grace given some in the world. They may have higher IQs. They may be better educated. They may have had better parents! Some of them grow up more emotionally healthy than those of us who may have been brought up with immature parents. In a sense all parents are dysfunctional. Nobody is perfect. But it is possible that a non-Christian could have been brought up in a home far less dysfunctional than some of us who did not have the best parents. We may have endured tragedies in our young lives—the death or illness of a parent, mistreatment or even abuse by someone in a position of trust or authority. God's grace helps us deal with these things, but they have an effect on us nonetheless.

My point is this. We must learn to accept our backgrounds and understand why we are the way we are. We must not be surprised if there are those in the world who have no knowledge of the Lord Jesus Christ but who have very desirable temperaments. This would explain the lady in our supermarket. My old friend and mentor Dr. William Greathouse, now in heaven, had one of the most Christlike temperaments of anybody I have ever known. But I suspect he would have been much the same in his personality had he never been converted.

> *The difference between the Christian and the*
> *non-Christian is this: we have the Holy Spirit;*
> *they don't. They have their gifts and talents and*
> *learning without the Holy Spirit. We have our*
> *gifts and talents and learning plus the Holy Spirit.*

According to the ancient Greek philosopher Hippocrates (d. 370 BC), all humankind has one of the following four temperaments: melancholy (with a proneness to being sad or depressed), sanguine (lively, talkative), choleric (controlling, domineering) and phlegmatic (laid back and gentle). Granted there is some truth in this, I am not eager to defend this perspective. My point in mentioning this is that our personalities tend not to change. So a choleric person who becomes a Christian will be choleric following their conversion.

Conversion will not turn a choleric into a phlegmatic personality. A person who is by nature melancholy will not become sanguine because they are saved. Conversion to Christ will not raise your IQ. If you preferred science to the arts before you were saved, you will still be more interested in astronomy, biology, or botany than you are in music, philosophy, and literature after you become a Christian. God will use your background to make you the kind of servant He wants you to be.

Where does pigeon religion enter in? Answer: *one can depend on his or her natural ability and suppose it is the Holy Spirit when it isn't!* If the Holy Spirit were completely withdrawn from the church today, 90 percent of the work of the church would go on as if nothing happened!

How do we explain this? Common grace. Common grace at work in the church without the Holy Spirit is pigeon religion. Pigeons easily become dependent on man for food. This is why pigeons congregate in public squares or wherever there are a lot of people. They love to eat what people have thrown away.

As a barracuda looks like a bonefish, a pigeon looks like a dove, so people with a certain charisma can appear to have the genuine anointing.

One might say, just maybe, that common grace is the most benign form of pigeon religion. And yet it could be the most dangerous! Why? We tend to depend upon our natural ability. It becomes the flesh, not the Spirit. After all, people with great talent and influence can get things done! One might be persuaded to think it is the anointing! But common grace is sometimes capable of imitating the Holy Spirit.

As a barracuda looks like a bonefish, a pigeon looks like a dove, so people with a certain charisma can appear to have the genuine anointing. It reminds me of the recent comment from a Chinese pastor, having been given a tour of American churches: "I am amazed at how much the church in America can accomplish without the Holy Spirit."[1]

You might argue that "common grace" is also of God. True. But the church was never meant to be empowered by creation gifts. When Jesus promised that the disciples would receive "power" (Luke 24:49; Acts 1:8), it was not a reference to natural gifts. Peter by nature showed himself to be a coward when he denied knowing Jesus (Matt. 26:74). But on the Day of Pentecost he was as bold as a lion: utterly fearless and full of confidence (Acts 2:14–39).

THE EFFECTS OF COMMON GRACE

Common grace, then, can produce the following without the immediate and direct witness of the Holy Spirit:

1. *Charisma.* This is a pure Greek word. It means gift of grace. One might therefore hastily infer that charisma and the anointing are the same. Not true. People like Winston Churchill, Bill Clinton, Barack Obama, and Donald Trump are full to overflowing with charisma. It is gift of

grace—common grace. Charisma is a compelling attractiveness or charm that can inspire devotion in others. It is truly a divinely conferred power or talent—no doubt about it. But it is not the consequence of the immediate and direct power of the Holy Spirit. It is a creation gift. Some leaders have it, some don't. To those who have it there is to be seen an amazing ability to inspire devotion.

Adolf Hitler had it. Charisma is therefore a gift that can be abused, twisted, and perverted to persuade people to do evil. Likewise there are ministers who have this charisma, and if they are not truly godly and devoted to the glory of Christ, they can lead sincere people astray. And yet somewhere in between the Hitlers and Trumps of this world are countless pastors and teachers who have pleasing personalities that cause their following to be loyal and devoted.

This of course does not mean that God cannot or will not use charisma for His glory. Like musicianship or any breadth of knowledge, God can use these for His glory. And yet one need not feel impoverished if they don't have it.

2. *Natural talent.* The ability to write plays or sonnets, like William Shakespeare; the mind that can compose concertos or symphonies like Edward Grieg or Ludwig van Beethoven; the ingenuity that can conceive of a St. Paul's cathedral in London or a Sheldonian Theatre in Oxford like Christopher Wren; the brain that could conceive the theory of relativity like Albert Einstein. These are gifts of God. The world is all the better for these. But there is little if any evidence that most of these men were Christians.

Therefore, when people with these abilities become a part of the church, the danger is that one might ascribe the Holy Spirit's enablement to people like them. People can make a profession of faith without having been regenerated. Or they might even be regenerate but still carry on in their own strength without the direct leadership of the Holy Spirit. Joseph and Mary went a day's journey without the child Jesus, having assumed He was with them all along (Luke 2:44).

3. *Natural intelligence* or *intellect.* There is a distinction between intelligence (the ability to grasp quickly) and intellect (the ability to amass knowledge). In either case one must see these as gifts of common grace. When people with massive intelligence or intellectual aptitude become a part of the church, it is so easy to impute the Holy Spirit's power to them when they make suggestions. Also, when people like this get into the leadership of the church, the temptation for them is either to take over or assume their wisdom is from God. It could be, but maybe not.

Because people can be so brilliant in their areas of expertise, ordinary church members often assume that when the former speak it must be the mind of Christ. I have watched situations in which very able people speak up—and all listen and acquiesce—only later to find out that their opinions have been utterly wrong. The pigeon can light on the most brilliant mind and cause havoc among the people of God.

4. *Education.* This of course borders on what we have said above. But it must be added how the educated often intimidate those who have not had the privilege of a good education. It is also often assumed that educated people must be so apt and wise in their judgments. Sometimes this is true, but not always.

This is why the teaching of the ungrieved Spirit of God needs to be grasped and applied. If the educated and the learned would embrace this teaching and apply it to themselves, there is great hope that pigeon religion would not enter the church. This means living in total forgiveness, not pointing the finger, and waiting for the impulse of the Spirit in order to sense His opinion in a special situation. Intelligence or education will not bring this about; only humility and obedience to the ways of the Holy Spirit will.

5. *Preparation.* By this I mean the process of being made ready or available for a particular task. This often means hard work. This means faithfulness. For this reason, if one is

not careful he or she will assume they are ready and qualified to say certain things, to make particular judgments.

Take sermon preparation, for example. I can work for hours in preparing a sermon. I might therefore assume that when I speak it will be a good sermon. Sometimes it is, sometimes it isn't. I know what it is to be prepared well and do a poor job when preaching. Preparation is important, but it isn't everything. I'm not sure who said it first: prepare as if there were no Holy Ghost (in other words, work hard as if it were all up to you); preach as though you had not prepared (leaning totally on the Holy Spirit). That said, a highly gifted speaker could do so well that one could hardly tell the difference between the anointing and the counterfeit.

6. *Culture.* We all have a measure of culture. On a scale of one to ten, some are more "cultured" than others. It refers to habit, behavior, social intelligence, cumulative deposit of knowledge, the totality of one's learning, and sometimes, a particular appreciation of the arts, especially music. It is inevitably affected by one's geographical location. I live in the Nashville area—a town known for country music and especially "bluegrass." The Grand Ole Opry is the polar opposite of the Grand Opera of New York City. Both are cultures.

Pigeon religion enters this area when it is thought that one's culture is better than another's. Those who love art and music tend to look down their noses at country music. But those who love bluegrass music and the sound of a banjo sometimes think their culture is more godly! That could be the Cane Ridge influence. And yet lovers of Mozart show their pigeon religion by an equally superior attitude toward all others.

7. *Administrative gift.* One of the spiritual gifts is "administrating" (1 Cor. 12:28, ESV). But one can have this at the natural level. It is a great gift. It has been observed that John Wesley had this gift. Many of the conversions in English Methodism came from the preaching of George Whitefield.

But Wesley's gift of administration and organization enabled him to hold on to his and Whitefield's converts.

Organization is part of the phenomena behind the premise that the church continues on without the Holy Spirit. A church can be so well oiled and organized that the sheer machinery might hold it together and create the platform for growth. God can certainly use this—or there would not be a gift of administration. But one must nonetheless be aware that the Holy Spirit could be withdrawn and people would not know the difference.

I feel I must bring this chapter to a close by saying it is a sad day for the church when common grace replaces God's sovereign grace as the chief source for its ongoing existence. It is accomplishing so much, but without God—that is, without His special, sovereign grace. Jesus addressed this condition:

> I know your works: you are neither cold nor hot. Would that you were either cold or hot! So, because you are lukewarm, and neither hot nor cold, I will spit you out of my mouth. For you say, I am rich, I have prospered, and I need nothing, not realizing that you are wretched, pitiable, poor, blind, and naked.
> —Revelation 3:15–17, esv

A lukewarm church is one that has become virtually powerless by pigeon religion. Its success in many parts of the world is undoubted. But it has a natural explanation. That is not the way the church was supposed to exist. Yes, we do thank God for common grace. Where would we be without it? Where would the world be without it? And yet it was never meant to be the driving force of the church of Jesus Christ in the world. We may want to say, "But this is better than no grace at all." Not so, according to Jesus; He wants us either cold or hot!

A typical lukewarm church says, "We have need of nothing. We are absolutely fine the way we are." This makes Jesus sick; He wants to spit a lukewarm church out of His mouth!

My Memorable Climb-Down

But perhaps there is something worse than that, namely, feeling that we *deserve* the blessing of the Holy Spirit. God hates this. And yet I was so guilty of this when at Westminster Chapel. One evening I heard about a "Toronto Blessing" taking place at Holy Trinity Brompton, a leading Anglican church in London. It was claimed that the Holy Spirit had fallen on those people big time!

"No," I said. "If what is happening there were truly of God, it would have come to Westminster Chapel first!" After all, *we* had borne the heat of the day. *We* had fasted and prayed. *We* broke tradition and sang choruses and gave altar calls, putting my ministry on the line. What is more, *we* were out on the streets witnessing to the lost.

Not only that; surely God would not bless Holy Trinity—an Anglican church. "We all know that the Church of England is apostate," I said to myself. "And half the staff are old Etonians with their posh accents. God would not bless people like that."

But I was wrong. So wrong. My attitude then was pure vintage pigeon religion (if there is such a vintage like that). I had to climb down—publicly—after warning my congregation that what was happening at HTB was not from God. I went on record that day that what was happening at Holy Trinity Brompton was a genuine move of the Holy Spirit. We prayed publicly for HTB and their vicar Sandy Millar. We never looked back. It was possibly the best climb-down I've ever made! My pigeon religion was transcended by the Dove.

So then, as I have been saying, it is not always easy to recognize the difference between a pigeon and a dove. Between a barracuda and a bonefish. Between the counterfeit and the genuine Holy Spirit. But such insight, were God to give it to us, is more valuable than gold.

Don't settle for pigeon religion. Wait for the real to come. God will show up to those who won't give up. His coming is worth waiting for.

CONCLUSION

Get wisdom! Get understanding!...Do not forsake her, and she will preserve you; love her, and she will keep you. Wisdom is principal; therefore get wisdom. And with all your getting, get understanding.

—PROVERBS 4:5–7

————————◆————————

**Pigeons fly high—a thousand feet or higher.
Doves fly no more than thirty feet high.**

————————————

THERE IS A cost if we are successfully to avoid pigeon religion. The way of the Holy Spirit is not always easy. Whereas we are given a wonderful freedom by walking in the Spirit, there is also self-discipline that God gives and which He expects us to use. The Christian life is a fight— spiritual warfare. And yet as we walk in the light, we have fellowship with the Father and enjoy the cleansing of the blood of Christ from all sin (1 John 1:7). Walking in the light means to welcome anything God shows us—whether it be new insight or a reminder of things we may have forgotten. And so the Christian walk is a fight, yes; but neither do we need to be afraid of the devil. Pigeon religion is having a greater fear of Satan than of God!

The reason that pigeons fly high, says Pete Cantrell, is to get away from hawks. They fly high for protection. "And yet I have never seen a hawk come down on a dove," who never flies more than thirty feet high. But why not? I ask. As to what analogy we may learn from this, perhaps it is this: if we are like doves, we don't need to be fearful of the evil one. "Whoever has been born of God guards himself, and the wicked one cannot touch him" (1 John 5:18). God has not given us a spirit of fear, or timidity, but "of power, and love, and self-control" (2 Tim. 1:7).

Are you willing to bear the cost of the unfeigned presence of the Dove? Are you willing to reject pigeon religion even if it costs you?

Whereas we are given a wonderful freedom by walking in the Spirit, there is also self-discipline that God gives and which He expects us to use.

Pray this prayer:

Heavenly Father, I blush to think how many times I have grieved Your Holy Spirit. I am so sorry and so ashamed. I ask for Your forgiveness. I thank You for that wonderful promise in 1 John 1:9, that if we confess our sins You are faithful and just to forgive those sins and to cleanse us from all unrighteousness. I now ask You to grant me true repentance, that I will be changed from glory to glory by Your Holy Spirit. Grant me the will to accept my forgiveness and not to look back. I welcome Your ever-increasing anointing from this day forward. Thank You for Your patience with me. In Jesus's name, amen.

May the grace and blessing of the Triune God—Father, Son, and Holy Spirit—be with you all. Amen.

NOTES

---◆---

INTRODUCTION

1. C. S. Lewis, *God in the Dock* (Grand Rapids, MI: Eerdmans Publishing Co., 2014), 293.

CHAPTER 3
LEARNING THE HOLY SPIRIT'S WAYS

1. "The Average Christian Prays a Minute a Day; Prayer by the Faithful Helps Their Relationships," God Discussion, May 26, 2013, accessed January 14, 2015 http://www.goddiscussion .com/110131/the-average-christian-prays-a-minute-a-day -prayer-by-the-faithful-helps-their-relationships/.
2. Margaret J. Harris, "I Will Praise Him," 1898, accessed November 17, 2015, http://www.hymntime.com/tch/htm /i/w/i/iwillpra.htm. Public domain.
3. Johnson Oatman Jr., "Count Your Blessings," 1897, accessed November 17, 2015, http://library.timelesstruths.org/music /Count_Your_Blessings/. Public domain.
4. "10 Reasons Why Gratitude Is Healthy," Huffpost Healthy Living, November 22, 2012, accessed December 10, 2015, http://www.huffingtonpost.com/2014/07/21/gratitude-healthy -benefits_n_2147182.html.
5. Richard Baxter, "Ye Holy Angels Bright," 1681, accessed November 17, 2015, http://www.hymnary.org/text/ye_holy _angels_bright. Public domain.

CHAPTER 5
EVANGELICAL PIGEONS

1. C. S. Lewis, *Miracles* (New York: HarperOne, 2015), 217.
2. "Voltaire Quotes," GoodReads.com, accessed December 10, 2015, http://www.goodreads.com/quotes/177460-when-it-is -a-question-of-money-everybody-is-of.

CHAPTER 6
GREED

1. C. S. Lewis, *Mere Christianity* (New York: HarperOne, 2015), 134.

CHAPTER 7
THE HERD INSTINCT

1. William Cowper, "O for a Closer Walk With God," 1772, accessed November 17, 2015, http://www.hymntime.com/tch /htm/o/f/o/oforaclo.htm. Public domain.

CHAPTER 8
PLAYING THE GAME

1. William Cowper, "God Moves in a Mysterious Way," 1774, accessed November 17, 2015, http://library.timelesstruths.org /music/God_Moves_in_a_Mysterious_Way/. Public domain.

CHAPTER 10
THE CANE RIDGE REVIVAL: AMERICA'S SECOND GREAT AWAKENING

1. James Smith, *History of the Christian Church* (Nashville: Cumberland Presbyterian Office, 1835), 565–566.
2. Peter Marshall and David Manuel, *From Sea to Shining Sea: 1787–1837* (Grand Rapids, MI: Revell, 2009), 66, accessed January 14, 2016, http://tinyurl.com/zkm9j3a.
3. Paul K. Conkin, *Cane Ridge: America's Pentecost* (Madison, WI: University of Wisconsin Press, 1990), 73, accessed January 14, 2016, http://tinyurl.com/zn2ueew.
4. Ibid., 86.
5. Ibid., 89.
6. Ibid, 92.
7. D. Newell Williams, *Barton Stone: A Spiritual Biography* (St. Louis, MO: Chalice Press, 2000), 61.
8. Conkin, *Cane Ridge*, 95.
9. Ibid., 105.
10. Ibid., 60.
11. Hugh Thomson Kerr, *Famous Conversions: The Christian Experience* (Grand Rapids, MI: Eerdmans Publishing Co., 1994), 98.

12. Stephen Mansfield, *Lincoln's Battle With God* (Nashville: Thomas Nelson, 2012), 23.

CHAPTER 13
"GIVE ME THAT OLD-TIME RELIGION"

1. Wikipedia.org, s.v. "Old-Time Religion," accessed December 10, 2015, https://en.wikipedia.org/wiki/Old-Time_Religion.

CHAPTER 14
COMMON GRACE

1. Kevin Turner, "Why Isn't the American Church Experiencing Revival?" *Charisma*, January 9, 2013, accessed December 10, 2015, http://www.charismamag.com/spirit/revival/1474-why-isnt-the-american-church-growing.

CONNECT WITH US!

CHARISMA HOUSE

(Spiritual Growth)

 Facebook.com/CharismaHouse

 @CharismaHouse

Instagram.com/CharismaHouseBooks

SILOAM

(Health)

Pinterest.com/CharismaHouse

REALMS

(Fiction)

 Facebook.com/RealmsFiction